SCARE TACTIC
THE LIFE & FILMS OF WILLIAM CASTLE

John W. Law

Writers Club Press
San Jose   New York   Lincoln   Shanghai

Scare Tactic
The Life & Films of William Castle

Published by Writers Club Press
an imprint of iUniverse.com, Inc.

For information address:
iUniverse.com, Inc.
620 North 48th Street
Suite 201
Lincoln, NE 68504-3467
www.iuniverse.com

All photographs are part of the author's private collection.

ISBN: 0-595-09544-5

Printed in the United States of America

Dedicated to William Castle. His love of movies was visible through his artful promotion of them.

Contents

III—The Decline

IV—Analysis

Acknowledgements

It would be impossible to acknowledge all those who assisted, knowingly and unknowingly, in the production of this book. The back of this book lists a number of sources used in the research that resulted in what you see before you. The author gratefully thanks these resources, for the book would have not been possible without them. In particular, William Castle's autobiography, *Step Right Up—I'm Gonna Scare the Pants off America*, provided insight into the director/producer's recollections, and was invaluable as a reference. In addition, the author wishes to thank any and all who provided interviews offered comments, suggestions and insights that made the book come together. Special thanks goes out to my family, as well as Tom Moulton and Suzanne Stack, for their support and assistance. Thank you to the Cinema Shop in San Francisco for help gathering some of the photographs that complement the story chronicled here and to the Pacific Film Archives and Internet Movie Database for research assistance. In addition, thanks to Denise Noe, Shelly Jacobs, James Phoel, Michael Arnzen, Tom Weaver, Jeffrey Schwarz and John Waters for their help and interest in my project at various stages of its development. And finally, special thanks to Terry Castle, the daughter of William Castle, for her words of encouragement.

Introduction

As Hollywood and the industry of movie-making advances into its next century, the road traveled is littered with greats and not-so-greats. With talents that will live on forever, in the hearts and minds of moviegoers, and of those that glimmered briefly like the momentary light of a match, quickly blown out and soon forgotten.

So many actors, directors, writers, cameramen, production assistants, set designers, and countless others have taken part in the creation of film. Those who are well remembered will undoubtedly live on forever. Those who are not, well, they too will somehow live on, but, possibly, only in the shadows of the celluloid they helped create.

But film is more than moments captured on a thin strip of celluloid. It's an emotion and a thought, passed through the miracles of sight and sound, into an open mind that catches that moment and locks it away.

We as viewers of film often remember our lives through the tapestry of a cinematic history. We remember the stars and films of our childhood. The effect the death of Bambi's mother, or Old Yeller, had on us as a child. We remember the movies we saw on our first dates, or with our teen-age friends when our parents finally let us go alone, or in the loneliness of a rainy Saturday afternoon.

We also remember movies that affected us by touching our soul or showing us a view we'd never seen before. The opportunity to see the unfurling of the Civil War in *Gone With The Wind*, or the advent of the space age with *2001: A Space Odyssey*. The painful realities of war in *Platoon* or the struggle for truth and justice of *To Kill A Mockingbird*.

But not all film must be cinematic genius. It does not have to always make us think or touch upon the tragedy of the human condition. Sometimes, it merely needs to entertain.

The comedies, musicals, dramas, epics and sci-fi films transported us to worlds we'd never visited before and for a few hours let us remove ourselves from our own world and immerse ourselves in another, all the while knowing it was only a movie. Perhaps that's why we love to be scared at the movies.

The shadow through the shower curtain and the piercing violins as Janet Leigh meets her untimely end in *Psycho*. The gasps and gulps as a shark happens upon a crowd of carefree swimmers on a hot summer day in *Jaws*. Even Jason, monster that startles us as he bursts from the lake in the final moments of *Friday the 13th*, or the demonic voice of Linda Blair in *The Exorcist*, are sights and sounds we won't soon forget.

In the annals of horror few men have outlived the films they created. Of course there are the legends of on-screen greats like Lon Chaney and Bela Lugosi, but they are more remembered for the characters they gave life to. Alfred Hitchcock is well regarded for his impact on the genre of horror, but his legacy is far greater than that.

William Castle may very well be one of the few exceptions whose legacy of horror showmanship has outlived that of the works he created. His love of Hollywood was shown not through the films he directed or produced, but for his artful promotion of them. His contribution to the industry of film went beyond his films. Most were mediocre at best and are rarely, if ever, counted among the best Hollywood has offered. But Castle's contribution is noteworthy because he extended the filmgoing experience beyond what was happening on the screen. How the crowd reacted to the images there and their participation made each showing different. While some laughed at his fare of horror, others avidly participated in its scares, enjoying the movie-going experiences he offered.

Percepto, Emergo, Punishment Polls, Fright Breaks, and life insurance policies against death by fright brought the marketing of motion pictures to a new level. His on-screen appearances put a face to the movies he gave life to. He accepted the blame of failure and bad reviews just as he did the rewards of box office success. And he always tried to give his audience exactly what it expected. In time he had fan clubs across the country and a following of avid moviegoers who lined up to see his next gimmick.

It took many years for William Castle to find his niche in the rough and fickle world of Hollywood. A director of B features for Columbia, a stint as a dialogue director, and even as an actor, William Castle played the Hollywood game as best as he could. He never claimed to be a brilliant director. He long admired the work of Alfred Hitchcock and Orson Welles, and perhaps even hoped to direct with the same flair with which they did. But more than that, he longed to make his impact on the world of film and around 1958 he discovered that his best shot would be in trying to "scare the pants off America."

No one ever expected to see an Orson Welles or Alfred Hitchcock film when they walked into a William Castle movie. They hoped for some shocks, a few scares, and a few laughs in an entertaining night at the movies. They usually got what they were looking for.

As a master showman, William Castle left his mark by savoring the entire process of movie making. But by allowing his moviegoers to participate in the filmgoing experience he also offered them a chance to be a part of the movies. When Vincent Price screamed that *The Tingler* was loose in the theater, patrons were asked to scream for their lives and they loved it. Seeing a glowing skeleton emerge from the movie screen in *The House on Haunted Hill*, or using "viewers" to see the ghosts in *13 Ghosts*, allowed the movie and Castle to step off the screen and to become one with the audience. It was fun and Castle enjoyed it as much as the audience.

He never expected the critics to praise his movies and he probably never expected to win awards for his work. Some even suggest that his gimmicks may have lessened the quality of his work because they seemed to say the work itself wasn't strong enough to draw an audience, therefore he needed a promotion to get them through the door. Castle knew going in that he didn't have the money or the stars to garner attention at the box office, and found that gimmicks were his best shot at getting noticed. Castle himself once proclaimed, "There is no God but gimmick. And Castle is his prophet."

But his films live on. Revivals draw crowds as the movies and their gimmicks are dusted off and occasionally reintroduced to new audiences and old fans alike. Director Joe Dante, whose film *Matinee* was, in large part, inspired by the work of William Castle, says regardless of what the critics have said he was true to his audience. "I went to a lot of Castle films," said Dante. "I remember the cards for the Punishment Poll and the tickets for the Coward's Corner. He may never have made a great movie, but he made going a lot of fun."

His career was long and varied and while the coming chapters will attempt to paint a full picture of the man and his cinematic legacy, the wealth will be dedicated to the role he accepted in the late 1950s. With the release of *Macabre* in 1958, his foray into producing, directing and promoting of horror was followed by a series of films that earned him fame and fortune through a variety of gimmicks used to promote his films.

Broken into four distinctive sections, this book first chronicles the formative years of William Castle. From his childhood and his early years in the theater, to his budding career at Columbia Pictures, we see the evolution of William Castle as a filmmaker and the path that led him to his role of master showman.

The second section deals with the decade of his greatest success. From *Macabre* in 1958, to his biggest success as producer of *Rosemary's*

Baby in 1968, Castle attempted to carve his niche in Hollywood and it is this period that he is best remembered.

The third section of this book deals with the decline. From 1969 until his death in 1977, Castle continued to work in Hollywood struggling to recreate the success of his past.

The final section of this book offers an analysis of Castle's body of work and its impact on Hollywood. Films and filmmakers have been influenced by Castle's work, and his influence is still affecting Hollywood. Those issues are discussed as well as the various themes that found their way into Castle's work. Recurring images and events from his past often found their way into his work. Also included in this final section is a chronicle of the films of William Castle.

On a final note, William Castle's memoirs, first published in his 1976 book, *Step Right Up, I'm Gonna Scare the Pants off America*, offer the most extensive detail of the career of William Castle and provided invaluable assistance in researching this book. Castle's recollection of events and reactions to important moments in his career are an important part of the director/producer's story. However, Castle's own penchant for hyperbole colored various events in his life and, where possible, this book attempts to set the record straight. Until the very end, William Castle remained a master showman.

I

The Formative Years

Full Circle

When William Castle died in 1977 he was still shooting for the big time. In production with his next film, *200 Lakeview Drive*, Castle suffered a heart attack on Tuesday, May 31, 1977 and died later that evening at UCLA Medical Center. Hollywood didn't pay much attention and he never had the chance to finish the film.

Castle had, in many ways, come full circle. His early years in the industry were of little notice. Years spent toiling away directing small pictures that were rushed through production and quickly routed through theaters. Most of those films faded into movie history along with thousands of other films of little notoriety. He finally was noticed for his series of camp horror films with memorable promotions beginning in 1958 with *Macabre*. And after a decade of showmanship as Hollywood's master of gimmicks, Castle again faded into the backdrop with films that received little notice and even less return at the box office. He reached his peak as the producer of *Rosemary's Baby* in 1968 and no picture that followed could compete with the horror classic.

Had William Castle survived he might have seen a renaissance in his career or at least in the view of his contributions to the industry he loved so much. Revivals of his horror classics, along with their notorious gimmicks, continue to delight fans and his career was mirrored on the big screen in a film that paid tribute to his love of promotion.

Producer/Director William Castle at the height of his career.

The Beginning

Born on April 24, 1914 in New York, his name was William Schloss, Jr. He was an only son, but had a sister, Mildred, who was born 11 years earlier.

He claimed his first memory of being frightened and captivated by the world of horror was at the age of six when his father supposedly took him to see DeWolf Hopper in a stage production of "The Monster." It was here, he said, that he was in a state of such terror that he actually wet his pants. Castle may have been mistaken on his memories of this event because other reports say Hopper didn't star in the play until 1933. The show actually premiered in 1922 with Wilton Lackaye. Castle would have been about eight at the time.

The boy never liked the name Schloss, having to endure being teased in his early years as the other children called him names like "Schlupps," "Slush," and "Schlumps," he recalled years later. In addition, he said he was clumsy, awkward and withdrawn. The combination, he claimed, left him unable to participate in sports or make friends. It left him hating himself and as he once said, "I was good for nothing."

Around 1923, when he was nine years old, his parents sent him off to camp, possibly hoping he would break out of his awkward ways. But young Bill ended up in tears, fearing the idea. But Camp Pontiac turned into a blessing in disguise, claimed Castle, when he discovered a talent he didn't know he had.

In his memoirs, Castle wrote, "One afternoon, the boy in bunk number two looked at me with utter disdain. 'You're worth nothing, Slush, absolutely nothing.' The others loudly agreed. Silent, I sat on the edge of my bunk, feeling miserable. Then slowly I began to put my legs around my neck. I was double-jointed—My one claim to fame. When my feet touched behind my neck, I looked up in defiance. The boy in bunk number two gasped in awe. 'Look, Schlupps is a spider.' "

Castle added that a short time later, the camp held a circus in which he performed his newfound talent to thunderous applause, renewing his faith in life and in himself.

But around the age of 10 his life took a turn for the worse when his mother suddenly died of pneumonia and then a year later his father died of a heart attack. The trauma left young Bill scarred. It was a similar story to that of another famous director, Alfred Hitchcock. Hitchcock was about 15 when his father died suddenly. Both men, with their awkward childhoods and lack of father figures, were impacted immensely by their losses. Especially young Bill Schloss.

He claimed he was unable to cry at either of his parents' funerals. False bravado masked a frightened and confused boy. His sister, who was 22 at the time, was married in November 1926 and became young Bill's guardian. He moved in with Mildred and her new husband, Allan Klein, sleeping on the living room couch in their Manhattan apartment, but found growing up difficult. He developed what he claimed was a defensive covering, refusing to allow his family or anyone else to get close to him. However, his need for attention and affection manifested itself in death-defying stunts that were viewed as cries for help, although no one seemed to be listening.

In early 1926, when he was 11, he says he jumped into the Hudson River, determined to swim across. Onlookers screamed at the site, but young Bill continued to swim. Eventually his body began to cramp, but he had swam too far out to make it back to safety. He was certain he would die, he said. But in the nick of time, a river patrol boat came to his rescue, plucking the boy from the icy waters and saving his life.

Then, when he was 12, he leaped off the platform of the 116th Street Subway during rush hour. The crowd on the platform screamed as the subway car closed in on the young boy on the tracks, but fortunately it stopped in time and once again young Bill was saved from imminent death.

His sister and her husband did not know what to do with the boy, calling him "crazy" and pleading with him to "act like a normal boy." Bill responded by running away. He stole $30 from his sister's purse and decided to hitchhike to Hollywood with the doorman from his apartment building. The two made it as far as Albany when they decided to stop for the night. While Bill was asleep, his companion stole his wallet containing his $30 and disappeared. Bill awoke alone and found out he'd been ditched. He spent the next two days hitchhiking back to Manhattan with his tail between his legs. Afraid to face his sister, he slept outside the apartment building on a park bench. His sister found him there and allowed him back into her home. "What's to become of you, Bill?" she asked. "I'll think of something...I always do," he replied.

His First Taste of Horror

In 1927, when he was just 13 years old, young Bill Schloss again dipped into his sister's purse, stealing $1.10 to head to the theater to see Bela Lugosi in his Broadway stage production of "Dracula." Bill fell in love with the show and continued to steal ticket money from Mildred, and for two weeks he sat in the balcony every night watching the show.

He eventually worked up enough courage to head backstage to see the star. Telling the manager he was a friend of Lugosi's, he was miraculously allowed backstage and directed to the star's dressing room. He knocked at the door and was greeted by the deep, distinctive voice of the horror legend himself, allowing him to enter. Lugosi looked the boy up and down and asked, "What can I do for you, young man?"

"I've seen the play 12 times, sir," admitted starstruck young Bill. "And I think you're wonderful."

"Please sit down, Mr....?" motioned Lugosi.

"Schloss," replied the boy.

"Mr. Slush," continued Lugosi. "Would you like to watch the play from backstage tomorrow night?"

The boy was thrilled and quickly accepted the star's offer. It would be the first time he would have the opportunity to be behind the scenes of a horror classic. But certainly not the last. Bill discovered the place he felt most at home and happiest. But alas, it was only for one night. But Bill continued to return and every free chance he had was spent backstage with Lugosi's production. He loved every minute of it. Then it was over. The show ended its run in New York and everyone moved on, except Bill Schloss.

Disappointed and depressed, young Bill headed back into ordinary life, but at least he knew now he wanted to be a part of the theater. He just didn't know how it to make it happen. "I knew then what I wanted to do with my life," Castle wrote in his memoirs. "I wanted to scare the pants off audiences."

Within two years his big break came, Castle claimed, when, at the age of 15, a producer of the road company tour for "Dracula" called the young man and asked if he'd be interested in being an assistant stage manager for the show. Lugosi apparently remembered his young fan and recommended him for the spot. Castle immediately accepted and soon after dropped out of high school.

He found the opportunity one of the most thrilling in his life. Lugosi, he recalled, was both gentle and humble, far from the character he created on stage and film.

It was about this time young Bill decided he was due for a name change. Lugosi's pronouncement of "Mr. Slush" was the last straw and he knew he needed a better sir name if he was ever going to make it in Hollywood. He'd learned somewhere along the line that "Castle" was the English equivalent of his name and decide that would do. He renamed himself William Castle.

As assistant stage manager, the newly named William Castle dove into his work doing whatever was needed, and even offered his suggestions for packing in the crowds. Castle suggested several promotional gimmicks, including a closed black coffin outside the theaters and oriental incense that would create a mood for the audience. Neither of those ideas were accepted, however one of his gimmicks did find its way into the show.

Castle suggested that Count Dracula disappear in a cloud of smoke on stage and then suddenly reappear in the audience, giving the crowd a horrific shock. The stage manager thought the idea worthy and added it the show. The crowd enjoyed the stunt as the Count quickly appeared and then again would quickly vanish and reappear on stage.

Building a Career in the Theater

By the time he was 16, young Bill Castle was out of work. His stint as assistant manager on "Dracula" had come to an end and young Bill was out looking for work. It was the Depression and times were tough.

It's difficult to know how much money Castle had at the time. His father had provided for his children after his death and Castle would go on to inherit a considerable amount when he turned 25, but it's doubtful he would have left his son penniless on the streets of New York until he turned 25. However, Castle claimed in his memoirs that these early years were a struggle and he had to make his own way.

It was 1930 and Castle was desperately hunting for a job in the theater. To make ends meet he was washing dishes at an automat on 42nd Street. He was making a couple dollars a week and existing on whatever free food he received at work. Living in Greenwich Village, among scores of other artists struggling to make their way, Castle's home was a room on the fifth floor of a tenement-like building on MacDougal Street. The inhabitants shared a bathroom which was on the third floor and Castle was far behind on his rent, barely able to survive. Fortunately, as was the case with so many other starving artists in New York City during the Depression, Castle had a savior and his name was Albert Strunsky.

Strunsky was known as "The Village Landlord" and everyone affectionately referred to him as "Papa." Papa Strunsky fled to the United States from Russia when he was about 17. There he made his way, settling in Greenwich Village where he worked as a blacksmith long enough to make the money to purchase a small grocery store. The store prospered and soon Strunsky was purchasing land in the surrounding area and building apartment houses. His happiness and success was returned to the community by way of allowing the starving artists to live in his buildings, often rent free as they struggled to find success. Many did, including people like Eugene O'Neill and William Castle.

When they did they would repay Papa for his kindness. Castle, by the early 1930s owed him as much as $500, but Papa understood. He referred to Castle as "Simple Simon" and promised him that one day, he too would find success. He had undoubtedly said it many times and to many people. Castle believed him and didn't want to let him down.

In hopes of finding work in the theater, Castle would visit the offices of Broadway agents, theatrical managers and Actors Equity each day looking for work and viewing the listings of new shows that were currently casting. Trying his hand at acting, Castle noted that producer Jules Leventhal was staging a revival of "An American Tragedy" and several parts were currently being cast. Castle quickly got the number and called the production offices. Knowing every out-of-work actor in town would be auditioning for the play, Castle decided he'd need a gimmick to get through to the producer.

"Tell Mr. Leventhal that it's Samuel Goldwyn's nephew calling," Castle said to the receptionist, who immediately put him through to the producer. Continuing his bluff, Castle said his uncle suggested Leventhal might be able to find a part for him in his current play. Leventhal agreed to see him and Castle quickly headed to the theater where he pushed his way passed the crowd of hopeful actors and announced himself as Samuel Goldwyn's nephew. He explained the name change to Castle as his attempt at making his own way by not using the Goldwyn name and managed to get cast in a small part. The part actually ended up being five small parts with Castle using costumes and makeup to change his appearance. He was billed in three places as William Castle and used an alias for two other minor parts.

Life on the stage was good for young Bill. There were eight performances a week and he claimed that when he wasn't acting on stage, rehearsing his roles, or putting on makeup, he was watching the play from the wings or helping the stage manager backstage. He was learning all he could about the business.

Before he knew it, William Castle found himself cast in a new role when the stage manager quit the show and Castle was suddenly asked to take over. The evening before a young actress had seriously injured her hand in a mishap while waiting a curtain call. She put her hand on the ropes to the curtain while waiting her cue and when the stagehand pulled the ropes to lift the curtain the actress' hand was immediately dragged into the sharp prongs of the curtain pulley. Blood was everywhere and she was quickly rushed to the hospital where several fingers had to be removed. The stage manager was so upset he quit the play and Castle's knowledge of the production made him the best replacement for the job. He accepted, becoming, at the age of 16, the youngest stage manager in the history of Broadway, he claimed.

After the production's end, Castle managed to find more work in the theater, including a lead role opposite Marjorie Main in "Ebb Tide," as well as another lead in "No Small Frontier," and a part in a new version of "Oliver Twist."

But by 1934 the work became scarce. His sister Mildred, along with her husband and young daughter, had moved to Dallas where her husband was making his career in the dress business. Mildred had asked Bill to put his show business aspirations behind and come to Texas with them where he could work beside his brother-in-law, but Bill refused. At 20, he knew his life was in the theater and wanted to stay in New York. When the work stopped coming he again found himself penniless and living off the kindness of others like Papa Strunsky and wondering if he had made the right decision.

He managed to keep his head above water by giving impersonations of Hollywood stars like Lionel Barrymore and Edward G. Robinson each weekend at a small club called The Village Vanguard and during the summer he got a job aboard the SS Statendam, again giving impersonations of Hollywood stars. He also managed a variety of other small jobs to make ends meet, including a job as a social director and a brief stint as a salesman at Bloomingdales.

A Shot at Hollywood

Although William Castle claimed his first visit to Hollywood came in 1939, several reliable sources place Castle there in 1937, where his acting career in the movies actually began.

Castle apparently took a stab at stardom in 1937 and spent some time in Hollywood, appearing as an extra in three features. The American Film Institute lists Castle in Republic Pictures *It Could Happen to You,* and in two Universal films, *When Love is Young* and *The Man Who Cried Wolf.* In the latter, Castle was a customer at a box office.

It seems that no studio contract and a lack of steady work may have driven the young actor back to New York where he would receive an inheritance from his father's estate and get back to work on the stage.

Castle never mentioned this earlier trip to Hollywood in his autobiography, but claimed his next shot on the road to success would come from none other than Orson Welles, a man who Castle would always admire.

Crossing Paths
with Orson Welles

Castle's father had provided well for his children and according to the details of his estate, his only son was to receive his share after he reached the age of 25. Castle picked up a $10,000 check on his 25th birthday in 1939. He wasn't exactly sure how the money would be spent, but it was burning a hole in his pocket almost immediately.

For his 25th birthday, his girlfriend Pat, a sculptress also living in Greenwich Village, decided to give Castle a birthday party and invited a variety of friends from the theater and art circles. The party would change his life forever and give him the answer to what to do with his inherited wealth.

At the party that evening was a young actor named Everett Sloane. Sloane himself was of little note to Castle, but he was actually one of a small band of elite actors called the Mercury Players. The group was headed by Orson Welles and had caught the attention of Broadway for its original theatrical productions. Castle admired the work of Welles early on and would always look at Welles' career as something to shoot for. Whether acting, directing, or producing, Orson Welles was always at the top of his craft and Castle knew it.

Welles made quite a name for himself in the theater by this point and was about to do the same in Hollywood and Castle was eager to have a moment of the man's time. He believed he and Welles were kindred spirits with much in common.

Welles had a showplace for his Mercury Players in Connecticut called Stoney Creek Theatre where he often tested his plays before delivering them to Broadway. Castle longed to worked with the master.

During the conversation with Sloane that evening, Castle attempted to find out how he could reach Welles in hopes of working with him. When he learned of his forthcoming trip to Hollywood to prepare his first feature film, *Citizen Cane,* he asked what was going to happen to the theater. When he was told Welles intended to close the Connecticut theater, Castle decided he could follow in the master's footsteps and take over the showplace. He managed to pry Welles' telephone number out of Sloane and quickly headed found a phone to call.

"Hello, Mr. Welles, this is Mr. Castle. No, please, don't hang up. I'm a Broadway producer," began Castle.

He had yet to produce anything, but did manage to convince Welles to speak with him about the possibility of turning over his Stoney Creek Theatre to this budding producer. Welles agreed to meet with him the following day. Castle was thrilled.

After hanging up the phone, Castle looked up to see a beautiful young woman standing there. She was a young German actress named Ellen Schwanneke who had starred in a successful German film called *Maadchen in Uniform* and received rave reviews. Castle was fascinated with the young woman and the two spent the remainder of the night talking. She had left Germany, hating what Adolf Hitler was doing to her homeland, but found it difficult adjusting and finding acting work in the United States.

Castle, never one to let an opportunity to pass him by, immediately asked her to star in a new play he was producing for his new theater, although he had yet to make a deal, or even a plea, to Orson Welles. Neither did he have a play. But those were mere formalities for Castle. Schwanneke hesitated. "You are so fast, Herr Castle, I must see the play first before I commit myself," she replied.

Meeting Orson Welles

The following afternoon Castle appeared at Welles' office and waited an hour before he finally had his chance to discuss his offer with the Hollywood's newest boy wonder.

Welcomed into his spacious office, Castle sat down as Welles paced before him, chomping on his trademark cigar. "Do you smoke cigars?" bellowed Welles in his deep distinctive voice.

"Of course," replied Castle, although he never had, but would forever after use the cigar as a trademark of his own.

Castle recalled in his memoirs that he then stood and began to pace along with Welles, and as both smoked, Castle put forth his play for Stoney Creek.

"Why should I let you buy Stoney Creek?" asked Welles.

"Because we're both Taurus," Castle joked. When Welles laughed, Castle forged ahead with his proposition.

"I have money, but I know that isn't important to you. What is important is that I have talent. We're both the same age....I've been in show business since I was 15," Bill continued, listing his stage work. "My love for the theatre is just as great as yours."

Welles turned to face Castle, looking directly at him and said, "You got a deal, Castle." He then left the room. Castle had what he wanted. His deal with Welles gave him 10 weeks at Stoney Creek at a cost of $500 a week—half of his first inheritance check. Now he only needed a play.

The First William Castle Production

Bill Castle actually had a play in mind for his first production. It was called *Seventh Heaven* and was actually filmed in 1927 as a silent movie starring Janet Gaynor. Gaynor actually went on to win the first Best Actress Oscar for her performance in this and two other films that year and *Seventh Heaven* also earned Oscars for both its writer and director.

Castle felt it was the perfect vehicle to star his new protégé, Ellen Schwanneke. Castle now had his theater, his play and his star. But before he could begin a major problem arose.

Before he could sign the contract to acquire the rights to *Seventh Heaven*, Actors Equity called him to say he would be unable to use Ellen Schwanneke in his forthcoming production. "Why can't I use Schwanneke? She's a great actress and should be allowed to work in America," Castle complained.

He was informed that no foreigner was permitted to perform in summer stock because it takes employment opportunities away from American actors, and therefore Actors' Equity prohibits it. But there was a loophole.

If there was a play written specifically for the German actress in which only she could star, and the director could convince the board, Actors Equity might permit the actress to perform.

"Is that all?" Castle replied. "I have a play written especially for Miss Schwanneke. I got it in Germany last year. No American actress could possibly do it. It was tailored especially for the great Schwanneke's talents."

Castle had never been to Germany and certainly didn't have a play tailored to the actress' talents, but quickly began to create one in his mind.

"What is the name of the play?" asked a board member from Actors Equity.

"Das Ist Nicht Fur Kinder," lied Castle.

It was the only thing he could come up with on short notice, he claimed in his memoirs. Although he did not know German, his parents were of German descent occasionally used the phrase when they wanted to discuss something that wasn't for the children to hear. Translated, the title simply means "Not for Children."

"I guarantee it will be on Broadway in the fall," promised Castle. "It has 40 people in the cast. Think of all the work it will mean for all our good American actors. Maybe I'll write 10 more in, making it an even 50."

Castle was told to bring the play in for the board to review it. If they agreed, Castle would be permitted to produce his play.

"Yes, sir, I'll be here with the play," agreed Castle.

Now all he had to do was write it.

A New German Playwright Is Born

"It was 3 p.m. and there was no time to lose," Castle wrote in his memoirs. "Racing to my one room on Riverside Drive, I tried to figure what kind of play could be written by 12 p.m. Monday."

He initially wanted to write a horror play, of course, but his star had something different in mind. "There's enough horror in the world," she complained. "People want to laugh in the theatre, not be frightened."

Castle claimed that he started to write at 4 p.m. on Friday and 48 hours and six pots of coffee later he had crafted his first German play under the name Ludwig von Herschfeld. The play had 39 characters and a dog. It was a comedy that detailed the experiences of a young German girl arriving in America.

Castle may have had more time than he admitted, or he simply got his math wrong, but he claimed by Saturday, 24 hours after he began writing,—not 48 hours like he also wrote in his memoirs—he took the manuscript to his German-Jewish tailor, Hans, and asked him if his son would be willing to translate the play from English to German. Hans called to his son, Willie, from the back of the shop and asked. The young man agreed to do the translation for $10, but said it would take him a week. Castle said that would be too late and that he needed the play by Monday morning. For an extra $10 Willie agreed to stay up the entire night and get the play to Castle on Sunday.

By Sunday night Castle had the play. On Monday morning he went to the German consul in New York and claims he convinced a German vice-consul to make it look official by stamping a swastika on the cover and wrap the document in standard red ribbon. By now, "Das Ist Nicht fur Kinder" looked like the real thing. But Castle had one other idea to make it look convincing. On his way to Actors Equity he says he stopped in Central Park and threw the manuscript in a pile of trash and jumped up and down on it to dirty it up. He brushed it off and then lightly burned the corners, "just enough to make it look like it had come out of some bombed-out building in Europe," he said.

He made it to Actors Equity by noon and two hours later had permission to stage his play with Ellen Schwanneke.

Will Anyone Show up Opening Night?

The cast was easily assembled, Castle noted, and Stoney Creek was an excellent theatre. Welles had renovated the building and the cast and crew were housed in a large building about a block from the theatre, where they were fed and cared for by kind motherly woman, Castle added. Engraved invitations were sent out announcing the play, its star and producer.

By the second week of rehearsals not a single ticket had been sold and Castle was beginning to worry about having a full stage performing to an empty house. He had already spent his first $10,000 inheritance check on the theater, cast and production costs and needed to recoup his expenses if he were to stay in business. It was a hot summer and little was happening in Connecticut. In addition, the knowledge that Orson Welles and his Mercury Players were no longer on stage caused people to lose interest in Stoney Creek. And just when he thoughts things couldn't get worse, they did.

Rehearsals had broken early due to the heat and Castle was outside near the box office when he was approached by his star. "Bill, I must speak to you privately," she said. "Something terrible has happened."

"What's the matter Ellen? You're not ill?" Castle asked.

Schwanneke handed him a gold-embossed card written in German. "It's an invitation from Adolf Hitler to return to Germany," she explained.

Schwanneke told Castle that a German film festival was being planned and the festival would showcase all the great German stars, including Schwanneke. A letter and an invitation, signed by Dr. Joseph Goebbels, the Reichsminister of Propaganda and Enlightenment, said her presence was being requested by the Fuehrer. If she attended she'd have to leave the play.

The actress left Germany because of Hitler and told Castle that she had no family in Germany and did not like what was happening with her homeland. However, because it was beginning to look like her American debut was going to fail and it would be unlikely that she would find any more work in America, she feared she had no choice but to return to Germany. Castle asked her directly if she would like never to have to return to Germany, when she said yes he told her he would take care of everything.

"What are you going to do, Bill?" she asked.

"Wait and see, just wait. I think Adolf Hitler has brought us good luck…the dirty bastard!" Castle proclaimed.

Castle's flair for gimmicks had done him well thus far, so there was no need to stop here. First, he sent a cable. "Cable to Adolf Hitler, Munich, Germany," Castle told the woman behind the counter at Western Union. "Dear Mr. Hitler: Ellen Schwanneke turns down your invitation. She has positively said no. She wants nothing to do with you or your politics. She will not return to Germany as long as you remain in power. Signed, William Castle, Producer/Director, Stoney Creek Theatre, Connecticut. P.S. She's working for me now."

"Do you really want to send this?" the Western Union woman asked.

"Of course, and send another one of the same to Dr. Joseph Goebbels," Castle added.

Castle then had 20 copies of Schwanneke's letter and invitation and his reply cable made up and went to visit all the large daily newspaper editors he could think of in New York. He told them his star did not want any publicity, but explained to them his story as dramatically as he could, leaving behind a copy of the invitation and his reply cable.

Success with the Press

He knew the Hitler angle was perfect for the press and they did not disappoint him. He wrote in his memoirs that four major New York dailies carried the story on their front page the next day. "The Girl Who Said No to Hitler," "Stood Up Hitler, Banned on Nazi Stages," "German Actress Snubs Fuehrer," and "Fuehrer's Idea of Having Fun Isn't Schwanneke's" proclaimed the newspapers. The articles discussed Schwanneke's career and the new play. Some even reprinted the invitation and cable. Wire services also picked up the story and soon newspapers across the country were writing about the saga. Castle got noticed and a week before the play was set to open the show was sold out.

But Castle wouldn't leave well enough alone. He wanted to make a splash.

At 4 a.m., in the early morning hours of the day the play would open, Castle quietly went over to the theatre and overturned the box office, broke the windows painted swastikas on the walls with bright red paint.

At 8 a.m. he said he was awakened by the cast and crew who were shocked by what had happened and were beginning to panic about opening night. Castle assured them that the show would most definitely go on, even if he had to ask the governor of Connecticut to bring in the militia for protection. And that's exactly what he did. Soldiers surrounded the theatre and ticketholders were inspected to ensure safety to the performers. It was everything he had hoped for and more.

On hand to see Castle's debut play was Samuel Marks, an executive from Columbia Pictures. And soon, Castle was headed for Hollywood.

Go West Young Man

Columbia Pictures formally came into being in 1924 when Harry Cohn changed the name of the studio he had helped found along with the help of his older brother, Jack, and a friend, Joe Brandt. The Cohns and Brandt had originally started in the picture business at Universal, but ventured out onto their own with CBC, or Cohn-Brandt-Cohn, a motion picture company created to produce a series of short features called *Screen Snapshots,* which were both popular and inexpensive to make.

In 1922 the studio produced its first full-length film, *More To Be Pitied Than Scorned,* at a cost of $20,000. The success of the film gave the studio the clout it needed to become a major player in the movie business and led to the renaming of CBC as Columbia Pictures Corporation.

The studio managed to develop a few stars of its own in the later 1920s, including William Haines, Jack Holt and Barbara Stanwyck, and had the fortune of hiring a little-known director named Frank Capra. Capra directed a successful film called *Submarine,* in 1928, which was the first film to use sound effects. Success continued and by the mid-1930s the studio was releasing major films like Capra's Oscar-winning *It Happened One Night* (1934) and *The Awful Truth* (1937).

By the time William Castle was on his way to Hollywood, Columbia Pictures was well established as one of the major motion picture companies of its day and Castle knew it could be his shot at the big time.

Go West Young Man

It was the summer of 1939 when a young Bill Castle was noticed by Hollywood. His production of "Not For Children" caught the attention of Samuel Marks, an executive working for Harry Cohn and Columbia Pictures. Marks' search for talent was not a major priority for the studio. Columbia had very few leading directors, or stars for that matter, under contract in the early years. Often it borrowed major stars on loan from other studios and used the directorial talents of independent directors. Capra was an exception. Howard Hawks, John Ford and George Cukor provided the studio with major hits, but never under contract. Besides Capra, the only other major directorial talents under contract at Columbia was George Stevens.

But Marks must have seen a glimmer of talent in Castle and in the entire production at Stoney Creek that summer in 1939. Qualified directors and producers were needed in Hollywood to churn our smaller films that helped keep the studios afloat. A continuous flow of new material was needed in theaters to keep moviegoers coming back. Double bills of smaller films also attempted to draw in viewers. Directors and producers and a cast of other talented crew members were needed to keep the production costs down and on schedule.

Castle recalled in his memoirs that Marks stayed on after the end of the first show at Stoney Creek. He stayed with the theater group for several days while it prepared for its second show, "This Little Piggy Had None," a horror play about a man who suffers a mental breakdown because he looks like a pig.

During a break in rehearsal for the new play Marks asked Castle if he'd be interested in working for Columbia Pictures. "I thought you'd never ask," was Castle's enthusiastic reply.

"I can make no promises, but I think Harry Cohn will like you," explained Marks. "I think it's worth the gamble."

There apparently was no discussion of depth on Castle might actually do at Columbia, but Castle was ready for his shot at Hollywood and didn't give it much thought. "Remember, I can offer you nothing, only an introduction to Harry Cohn. But I'll tell him about the great work you've done here," emphasized Marks.

"Sam, I can be ready to leave in two weeks. Is that okay?" responded Castle.

Marks agreed to the time frame, which allowed Castle to finish the current play. However, he had to cancel plans for his next production, called *Dead End*.

Marks had business to attend to in New York and the two agreed to drive out to Hollywood together in Marks' car. But the following week Marks called and said he had to fly back to California immediately. He told Castle to drive the car out himself, but Castle didn't know how to drive. As a remedy, they put an ad in the paper to find someone who could drive and was trying to get to California. Castle recalled that over the next few days several people responded to the ad. He decided on a guy about his age named Charlie. When it was settled, Castle wired Marks, letting him know he was on his way and would see him in Hollywood in several days.

Castle had canceled plans for his next play, but had already purchased the props—several stage guns, including sawed-off shotguns, along with handcuffs, a blackjack and counterfeit money. He packed the items in his luggage, unsure of exactly what he would do with them. The two then headed off on the road to Hollywood.

Trouble on the Road

By the time they reached Cheyenne, Wyoming they were several days unshaved and wearing only jeans and sweatshirts, but were driving the expensive car of a Hollywood executive. Tired from a long day's drive, the pair decided to stop for the night.

Castle claimed in his memoirs that both men were unaware the modest-looking house they found to spend the night in what turned out to be a whorehouse. And shortly after they had settled down for the night, the men were surprised when women came in and climbed into bed with them and even more surprised when police burst into the house and arrested the two men.

Castle and Charlie were arrested, handcuffed and taken to the police station. When their belongings were searched the police found Castle's props from his unrealized play and they thought they had caught a big-time criminal. Castle claimed the police were actually searching for two hold-up men, which coincidentally fit their description. The men were locked up and Castle feared the key would be thrown away. When he was given his one phone call he called Sam Marks, but he wasn't home.

The men spent the next several days in prison. In addition to the prop guns, Castle didn't have the registration to Marks' car and the police believed it was stolen. Castled explained to the cops he was on his way to Hollywood to work for Harry Cohn and Columbia Pictures. The police called Columbia, and Castle said they even spoke with Cohn, but Cohn didn't recognize the name, so Bill and Charlie remained in jail.

Young Bill Castle hated his time behind bars. The food was impossible to eat, he developed red welts all over his body from bed bug bites after sleeping on the dirty mattress in his cell, and he found himself keeping company with men he feared.

One man, Castle claimed in his memoirs, rattled on and on about an unfaithful wife he had strangled. Castle later thought the idea might find its way into a movie of his someday—if he ever got to make any.

Free at Last

Harry Cohn was getting a shave from his studio barber in his luxurious office one afternoon, and while discussing business with Sam Marks, the subject of William Castle came up. "I wonder what happened to my car and Bill Castle?" supposedly asked Marks. "It's been two weeks since I heard from him."

Cohn looked up and said, "What'd you say the guy's name was?" "William Castle," replied Marks.

"The bum's in jail in Cheyenne, Wyoming," answered Cohn as he remembered the call from police he received several days earlier.

The studio called the jail and Castle said that from that time on he received V.I.P. treatment and he felt like a celebrity. When asked to sign a release letting the police off the hook for false arrest, Castle and his co-traveler Charlie gladly signed and were soon on their way. Three days later both men arrived in Hollywood on September 20, 1939. Castle dropped off the car and parted ways with Charlie, who was headed to San Francisco, and Castle checked into the cheapest hotel he could find near the Columbia Studios.

Sam Marks was supposed to call and tell him when to report to the studio and Castle waited at the hotel all day, checking the front desk for messages each half hour, but Marks didn't call.

Castle supposedly waited all day and when Marks still didn't phone he finally decided to venture outside to explore his new neighborhood—Hollywood.

It was evening when he claimed in his memoirs that he wandered past Grauman's Chinese Theatre on Hollywood Boulevard. It was there he said he ran into a pretty young redhead who told him she was Susan Hayward and that she had just had a screen test to play opposite Gary Cooper in *Beau Geste*. She said she was going to be a star and each wished the other good luck on their road to success while she stood in Jean Harlow's footprints and he in Lon Chaney's.

While it's certainly possible Castle and Hayward crossed paths during their early years in Hollywood, it's doubtful this September event actually transpired as Castle's memoirs claim. *Beau Geste* was released in August 1939, a month before the supposed meeting, and Hayward was already on her way to stardom, having signed a seven-year contract with Paramount Pictures earlier in the year.

The budding director says he returned to his hotel room later that evening and found a message waiting for him. Sam Marks had called and left a message. Bill Castle was to report to Columbia Studios at 11 a.m. the next morning where he was to meet with the legendary Harry Cohn.

The Columbia Years

Columbia was most definitely a powerhouse among Hollywood studios by the time William Castle first set foot inside Harry Cohn's finely-tuned movie-making machine.

For Columbia, its bread and butter was in serials. Although the studio did produce several major films each year, its attention was directed at low-budget film series and shorts. *Blondie, The Three Stooges* and *Boston Blackie* series titles were just three of note. The studio was not a major moneymaker among the big studios, but did manage to garner profits during most of its formative years. In 1939 however, the year the studio's star director, Frank Capra, left, the studio faced its least successful year financially. But, at the time Castle arrived on the scene, the studio was putting out more than 50 features a year.

Arriving at 10:30 a.m. for his 11 a.m. appointment with Cohn, the 25-year-old William Castle recalled that he was in "awe" at the sight of Loretta Young and Melvyn Douglas passing him at the reception desk as he waited for a pass and directions to the studio head's office. Young actually smiled at him and said good morning, he fondly remembered. Shortly after, he was on his way to meet his new boss.

Meeting the Boss

An outer office with three secretaries was followed by a reception room, where people visiting Cohn were instructed to wait until he was ready for them. Margaret Lee, Cohn's executive secretary, resided outside the doors to the legendary man's office, admitting or refusing visitors.

On this particular day Lee instructed Castle to take a seat and relax for a few minutes. Castle recalled that he was visibly nervous and Lee may have noticed. "Mr. Cohn's running late," she told him smiling. "Frank Capra's in there."

It's important to note here that Frank Capra's days at Columbia were coming to a close as William Castle arrived on the scene. Disagreements and legal battles between the studio and its leading director had severed the long relationship of Frank Capra and Harry Cohn. Capra had completed his final film for studio, *Mr. Smith Goes to Washington*, in late summer 1939 and the film was to be released that fall. Capra officially exited the studio in October 1939 and reports support that Capra had little to no contact with Cohn during his final days as the differences between the two men were too great. However, in Castle's defense, it is possible that he did have the opportunity to meet Capra on Columbia grounds during his final days there. It's just doubtful he met him outside of Harry Cohn's office.

Castle detailed in his memoirs that he was offered a cup of coffee and sat there waiting and thinking about the successful career of Capra. He only dreamed for success at the level of Capra's. "At that moment, the door opened and Frank Capra walked out. Standing up abruptly, I spilled the whole goddamn cup of coffee all over myself," wrote Castle.

Capra smiled and asked someone for a towel, telling Castle he'd help get him cleaned up, but before he had a chance he heard Cohn bellow, "Get your ass in here."

"You're a goddamn mess, Castle," Cohn muttered as he looked over the young man before him. Castle was speechless, saying only, "I spilled my coffee, sir."

"I can see that. For Christ's sake, sit down," instructed Cohn.

Castle took a seat in a chair before the studio chief's massive desk and looked around the expansive room. Roughly a dozen Oscars were displayed behind the desk, most of which were from Capra's films for the studio.

"Sam Marks tells me you might be Columbia material. Why do you want to work for Columbia?" demanded Cohn.

Castle, who would often refer to Cohn as "The Great Man," replied, "Because I want to learn everything there is about the motion picture business…I have talent…I'm…"

But before he could continue Cohn snapped, "Bullshit! I'll tell you when you have talent. Don't you ever tell me how good you are again."

Cohn then offered Castle a rare smile and explained that the studio was a tough place to work and he demanded a lot from his employees. Castle was given a trial contract of six months and if he survived that the studio had the option to sign him on for seven years. His salary was $50 a week. Young Bill Castle was finally in the movie business.

His contract was what Castle called, "a seven-way contract." He would have the opportunity to learn the film business from every angle—writer, director, producer, actor, production assistant, film editor and whatever other role was needed on a movie set. Or, in other words, they weren't really sure where Castle would fit in and decided to try his hand at everything to see what he was best at. And while Castle claimed it was a one-of-a-kind contract, it's doubtful that the studio gave any special attention to the young man from New York in designing his contract. His skills and talent were unknown at this point and he was one of thousands of Hollywood hopefuls struggling to make it in the business.

Working at Columbia

Castle spent the next several months learning his way around the studio and doing whatever tasks he was asked. He didn't do as much as he'd hoped and at times found himself bored.

Although there were no magnificent beginnings as director or producer, his first official production job is listed as dialogue director on
Columbia's *Music in My Heart*, starring Rita Hayworth, filmed in 1939
and released the next year. As dialogue director, Castle thought he
would actually direct the dialogue of the actors and help them get the
best out of their lines. He later found out that the role of a dialogue
director is actually that of apprentice director. His role was to occasionally cue actors and take care of minor details for the production. It
required him to get coffee, sandwiches and whatever else the director
might need.

In Castle's memoirs, he claims his first actual stint of dialogue director was for George Stevens' production of *Penny Serenade*, starring Cary
Grant and Irene Dunn. He recalled that he met Stevens at a diner near
the studio and asked if he could work for him.

The director admired Castle's enthusiasm and got him a job on the
set. Castle said the production began in December 1939 and detailed a
lengthy tale of his first experience with the legendary director of films
like *Alice Adams, Woman of the Year* and *The More the Merrier*. He
would later go onto make *Shane* and *Giant*. Castle may have been on the
set, and did recall specific details about Stevens' directorial style, however, other reliable reports show that production of *Penny Serenade* did
not take place until October 1940 and the film wasn't released until
1941. Therefore, it could not have been Columbia's most important
production in December 1939 as Castle claimed. And if Castle did work
on the film in any capacity it went uncredited and it would have been
more than a year after he had been hired by the studio.

Nevertheless, Castle began his early years at the studio working in
whatever capacity was asked of him. It's understandable that the wide
variety of his early experiences from his seven-way contract presented
him with an excellent understanding of the motion picture business at
all levels. He recalled working on as many as five films at the same time,
portraying a French gendarme in one film, a small bit as a doctor in

another, a dialogue director for another, and even working in the cutting room on another motion picture. He helped write his first film, *North To The Klondike*, a 1942 Universal release starring Broderick Crawford, and directed a short film called *Mr. Smug* that same year. His boredom phase was replaced by a busy schedule where he had little change to rest or enjoy life at a Hollywood studio.

A Directorial Debut to Forget

His first shot at directing came in 1942 when he was offered the chance to direct a film called *The Chance of a Lifetime*. Castle probably thought the title was perfect for him. Perhaps it was too good to be true.

At 28 years old, and having been with the studio for more than two years, Castle was longing to direct his first picture. The studio put out a number of B pictures each year and had a roster of lesser-known directors who churned out countless features under tight budgets and even tighter deadlines. Castle wanted his name on that list.

Pulling in $50 a week, Castle was living at a small apartment on the Sunset Strip, around the corner from Schwab's Drugstore, and managed to survive paycheck to paycheck. He wasn't living on steak and lobster, but at least he was working in the craft he loved. He befriended Cohn's studio chef, Andy, and one day helped him carry groceries into the private dining area. Only the invited were given the opportunity to dine with the studio chief and other executives and only the best was served there. Andy invited Castle into the kitchen and offered him a steak for lunch. Castle gladly accepted and soon found himself helping Andy as often as he could, in hopes of a free meal.

One afternoon, Castle said in his memoirs, he was eating in the executive dining room alone, sitting in Cohn's chair after Andy explained the room was closed for repainting. Not expecting to be interrupted, Castle was shocked when Cohn himself appeared, along with the other studio executives and demanded to know what he was doing there.

Andy had lied and the men sat down to dine with Castle. Castle claimed it was a ploy by the studio chief to play a trick on him after Andy had mentioned to Cohn that Castle had been helping him.

"So, Andy tells me you think you're ready to direct a picture," said Cohn. "He says every time he feeds you, you complain to him."

Andy agreed with Cohn and an embarrassed Castle began to realize the joke and before he knew it he was being given his first shot at directing a full-length motion picture.

Given Castle's penchant for stories, it's difficult to know how much truth there is to the story. Regardless, the resulting feature he was given was, in fact, *The Chance of a Lifetime.* "Let's find out if he's as great a director as he told Andy he was," said Cohn. Castle said Cohn had known for weeks he had been eating there and had decided it was time to let him direct. He wanted to deliver the good news along with a good scare.

As excited as he was about the opportunity to direct, Castle said that he found the script for *The Chance of a Lifetime* to be "dull, contrived and miserable." He said that he had suggested a rewrite, but was told he was to direct the film exactly as the script suggested and to not change a single line. Instead of telling Cohn the script was lousy, Castle thanked him for the opportunity to direct the film and set forth on making the picture. Location meetings, casting sessions, costumes, effects and so on kept the budding director busy for two weeks and at last he was ready to begin filming.

Chester Morris and Jeanne Bates were the two lead actors cast in the film and Castle wrote that on the first day of shooting, "I walked on the set with head high, as though I were going to direct *Gone With The Wind.*"

Well, *Gone With The Wind*, it was not.

Castle viewed the first cut of the final picture with Irving Briskin, one of Columbia's top brass. "It's a piece of shit!" uttered Briskin when the light came up in the screening room.

To assist him in saving the picture, Castle says Briskin put the end of the film at the beginning and edited sections of reel four into reel two and part of reel two into reel four, and so on. In the end, Castle says the picture became even more confusing than it was in the first place. When the picture finally was released in 1943 it was labeled a bomb. *Variety* said "*The Chance of a Lifetime* has one claim to fame—it's probably the worst directed picture in the history of motion pictures" and the *Hollywood Reporter* wrote, "William Castle, in his directorial debut, proves he is totally unfit to handle a motion picture—any picture."

Before the wounded director could escape the studio, a guard at the gate instructed him that Cohn wished to see him. The director feared the worst as he headed to the studio chief's office.

"Did ya read the reviews, Castle?" asked Cohn.

"Yes, sir," replied Castle.

"And whadja think of 'em?" asked Cohn.

"They weren't very good," he responded.

"Christ, I've read some bad ones, but these are probably the worst."

Castle wrote in his memoirs that he thought he was going to cry, but before he could Cohn told him to sit down and explained that they were lousy critics. "If they had any goddamn talent, they wouldn't be lousy critics," he explained. "How dare they question my judgment. If I say you're a good director, then goddammit, you're a good director, and nobody's going to change my mind except me!"

Cohn then told Castle he knew the script was a piece of shit in the first place. Castle's memoirs don't explain why Cohn wanted to make the film in the first place, especially if he knew it was going to be lousy, but he let the first-time director off the hook and offered him another chance. Actually, Castle was already working on *Klondike Kate*, a western starring Ann Savage and Tom Neal. But his next picture would be more suitable to the director's taste and would help renew Cohn's faith in the director.

The Whistler

Before Cohn had finished explaining to Castle his thoughts on movie critics he handed him a script and announced, "Your next picture. Read it, and when you've finished, call me at home and let me know how you like it."

Castle said he read the script three times before calling Cohn and saying, "It's horrific, Mr. Cohn...Exactly what I've been waiting for."

Released in 1944, *The Whistler* starred Richard Dix and J. Carrol Naish, both veteran actors that Castle had reservations about working with. Not because of their acting ability, but because they were so experienced, Castle feared his inexperience would make it difficult for the actors to take his direction. It apparently was not a problem.

The story revolves around a man, played by Dix, who is haunted by the death of his wife. He suspects that his friends believe he was responsible for her death and he cannot face living. Unable to commit suicide, the man hires a killer, played by J. Carrol Naish, to put him out of his misery. When Dix finds out that his wife is still alive he tries to contact the killer and stop his own murder, but he doesn't know who his killer is or when it's to take place.

For filming, Castle tried to think of every effect that would help add terror to the film. He said the actors admired his originality and were willing to follow his suggestions. One idea to increase the star's nervousness and fear was to have him give up smoking and go on a diet during production. He also would ask Dix to perform a scene over and over again, until he seemed almost desperate. And in the end it achieved the effect he was hoping for.

After viewing the finished film, Castle recalled that Cohn thought the film showed promise. "You're learning," he said.

Castle did admit that Cohn offered several important suggestions for improving the film and Castle followed his instructions.

The director had his own idea for improving the film, he noted. "That evening I suggested having some sort of gimmick at the audience level. We could have an actor dressed like the character Richard Dix played, run up the aisle of the theater screaming and have several plants in the audience faint."

Cohn turned the director down, but Castle told himself that one day he'd use a gimmick to promote a motion picture.

Favorable Critics

After its release in 1944, *The Whistler* received strong reviews and Castle was renewed in his talent as a director. *The Daily News* said his direction was "brilliant," and "the audience's attention is riveted to the screen throughout."

One critic even offered Castle what he might have considered the ultimate compliment. "Director William Castle has taken this material and molded it coolly and deliberately into many shapes of suspense. He has cut the dialogue down to a minimum and, a la Hitchcock, substitutes meaningful action and props…"

Castle was delighted with the reviews and thrilled to be compared to Alfred Hitchcock, a man whose career Castle obviously admired and longed to equal. But like most B films, the movie was quickly shepherded through the theater circuit and forgotten, never receiving the treatment of a Hitchcock picture. The film even earned a New York Film Critics Award in 1944. But Castle was already busy with his next project. He directed a sequel to the film called *The Mark of the Whistler* and a war picture entitled *She's a Soldier, Too*, starring a young Lloyd Bridges.

Cohn helped keep his movie empire afloat by loaning out his contract employees to other studios. Most major studios operated this way. Cohn could loan out a director or actor for ten times what he was paying them. He put Castle on loan for his next picture to the King brothers.

Hymie, Frank and Maurie King had recently arrived from Chicago to make their way in the movie business. They had sold their vending-machine business in hopes of being movie moguls. And while they never reached the level of a Harry Cohn or Samuel Goldwyn, the brothers did manage to produce a number of pictures during their years in Hollywood under the studio name Monogram. Castle was hired to direct Robert Mitchum in *When Strangers Marry*.

Between 1944 and 1947 Castle directed two more films in *The Whistler* series, *Voice of the Whistler* and *The Mysterious Intruder*, as well as several other series films, including *The Crime Doctor's Warning*, which was a series of 10 films, of which Castle directed four. Castle's contract with Columbia would end in 1947, however, in 1946 he stepped into the role of associate producer at the studio and crossed paths once again with a man he long admired—Orson Welles.

Orson Welles and Wedding Bells

During the release of *The Whister*, Castle received a call from a Broadway producer who had seen the film and wanted the director to direct a new play. The suspense genre quickly became Castle's passion and the play, entitled "Meet a Body," offered the same thrills and scares, but on a stage before a live audience. Castle approached Cohn and asked him if he could head to New York for the play.

William Castle claimed that Cohn told him David O. Selznick has asked to buy his contract, but Cohn refused. While the scenario is unlikely, the opportunity to work for Selznick at MGM would have been a great one, giving him a chance to direct A pictures, similar to those Hitchcock was doing. He claimed he was infuriated at Cohn's denying him this opportunity. To placate him, Cohn reportedly gave Castle his wish of heading to New York to direct "Meet a Body."

Castle soon headed to New York and back to the theater. He claimed he was taken off contract with Columbia for the six weeks he would be away and the play offered him $6,000 and a slice of the royalties. It was September 1944 and the play was set to open on October 2 at the Forrest Theatre, but first it opened in Boston to test audience response.

The Opening

"Meet a Body" took place in a Lower East Side funeral home. A man comes in to the funeral parlor and picks out a coffin and arranges a funeral for himself. As soon as the man exits the stage a shot is heard and moments later the man staggers back onto the stage and dies. The remainder of the play stages a whodunit and in the end the audience finds out who the killer is.

The play received strong reviews in Boston and Castle once again tried his hand at a gimmick. In the final act the killer jumped from the stage and running through audience as police chase him and a shoot-out occurs.

In New York, reviewers were not as kind and most said the play should be buried. To draw audiences, Castle reportedly took out ads in the obituary section of New York newspapers and managed to keep the play open despite the critics.

A Movie Idea Is Born

While in New York, Castle's completed film *When Strangers Marry*, opened and reviews again applauded the director. Even Orson Welles, who wrote a column for the *New York Graphic* said that for a B picture it was "one of the most gripping and effective pictures of the year."

During his stay in New York, Castle claimed an old friend gave him a copy of a book called *If I Die Before I Wake*, telling him it would make a fantastic movie. Castle read the book and agreed. Soon he tracked down the agent who owned the rights to the book and purchased the rights for $400, $200 up front and the remainder when and if he started filming.

Castle wrote up a 10-page treatment for turning the book into a film and when he got back to the studio he gave it to the story editor who turned the idea down. "Why?" Castle asked.

"The leading lady is a murderess," he replied. "Mr. Cohn likes his heroines good, sweet and pure."

Castle claimed he sent the book and treatment to Orson Welles with a note about the possibility of the two men working together and Welles agreed the story would make and excellent film. Unable to sell the idea to Columbia, Castle was out of luck, because his contract prohibited him from selling it elsewhere, as anything he did was actually owned by the studio. But this didn't stop Orson Welles.

Welles approached Cohn himself with a treatment for the book and Cohn jumped at the chance to have Orson Welles making a Columbia picture. And Rita Hayworth, Welles' new wife and one of Columbia's biggest stars, would play the lead. Cohn paid Welles $150,000 for the film, which Welles would direct. As an offering to Castle for finding the story, he was given the role of associate producer. The film was renamed *The Lady From Shanghai.*

This story about the origins of *The Lady From Shanghai*, again, may not be the full story, but only Castle's version of it. David Thompson, author of *Rosebud,* a biography of Orson Welles, researched the subject for his book and claimed that Castle actually bought the rights to the book shortly after it appeared in print in 1938. Castle reportedly then sold those rights to Columbia on conditions that if a film was ever to be made he would somehow be involved in its production. Castle did produce a treatment for the film and did send it to Welles who was interested in making the picture and inked a deal with Columbia to direct it. Cohn's interest in having a director like Welles working for the studio would easily have taken precedence over Castle's wishes to make the picture. But because of the contract, Castle had to be given a role in the making and associate producer would have been an obvious choice.

Before production began, Castle completed another film for Columbia, *The Crime Doctor's Gamble,* another mediocre B picture that Castle was quickly beginning to tire of.

Now regarded as a classic film noir feature, *The Lady From Shanghai* actually became one of the most expensive motion pictures of its time. Budgeted at $2.3 million, the picture was filmed on location in Mexico and aboard Errol Flyn's Yacht, the *Zaca,* which was used for many of the scenes at a cost of $1,500 a day. Castle enjoyed the opportunity to work alongside Welles, but found the production difficult at best.

Oppressive heat, rough waters and sickness nearly ruined the film and sent Castle into the hospital. He remained behind when the production wrapped and Welles and crew returned to Hollywood. Castle's job was to shoot additional close-ups of insects, iguanas, snakes and other jungle life. Castle became sick from parasites in the Mexican water that ate away at his stomach and returned to Hollywood only to spend weeks at the Cedars of Lebanon Hospital in Hollywood recovering. He lost 35 pounds before fully recovering.

When *The Lady from Shanghai* was released in 1948, it bombed at the box office. Fortunately, it was Orson Welles' bomb and not William Castle's.

Castle Takes a Wife

Back at Columbia, Castle's directorial efforts remained at the B-picture level. *Boston Blackie's Return* was followed by *The Lone Wolf's Revenge*. When he was given the script to *The Crime Doctor's Secret*, another sequel in *The Crime Doctor's Warning* series, Castle refused to direct the feature. He claimed the studio suspended him on November 28, 1947.

It's important to note that Castle's original contract with Columbia carried him into 1947, at which time Columbia may have renewed his contact and the director felt happy enough, even with his string of B pictures, to sign on again with the studio. Had David O. Selznick actually been interested in Castle, this would have been his chance to negotiate a deal, however, nothing ever happened.

Once suspended, Castle was unable to work for another studio because of the stipulations in his Columbia contract, which was very common in Hollywood. Out of work and out of a weekly paycheck Castle used his credit to treat himself to dinner one evening when he spotted a beautiful young woman sitting with an actor acquaintance of his. Castle worked his way up to the table to say hello to the man, Lowell

Gilmore, and hoped for an introduction to his attractive companion. "Miss Ruth Falck, this is William Castle. He's a director," said Gilmore.

Castle told the young woman, "You are indeed beautiful, Miss Falck....I wish you had a twin at home like you."

Mr. Castle, I do have a twin at home...who looks exactly like me," she responded.

Amazed at his good fortune, Castle suggested the four double-date and before he knew it he was at her doorstep. Ellen Falck and William Castle were soon face to face. "Which one am I, Bill?" she asked as she opened the door. "You're Ellen," he guessed correctly.

"I know it sounds corny," wrote Castle in his memoirs, "but if it is possible to fall in love at first sight, that night I did."

Castle claimed he remained on suspension from the studio for a month. He dined often with Ellen's family and dodged the rent as best he could. He proposed marriage to Ellen and she accepted. Castle then decided he had no choice but to honor his contract and head back to work. But Castle claimed that Cohn had heard about the engagement and demanded he meet Ellen. He approved and urged Castle to marry her before she changed her mind. As a wedding present, Cohn supposedly took Castle off suspension and the director went back to work. During this time he directed several features, including *The Gentleman From Nowhere* and *Texas, Brooklyn, and Heaven.*

Ellen and Bill were married on March 21, 1948 and as another wedding present, Cohn gave them a honeymoon in Europe, all expenses paid by the studio. The vacation was scheduled for June because Harry Cohn wanted Castle to do a small favor for him.

During the month-long honeymoon, Columbia asked Castle to direct second-unit filming of actors' doubles and authentic shots of Paris. Castle did the filming and headed off to enjoy his vacation, but as soon as they reached Rome, a wire from Cohn requested that he return to Hollywood for a picture. Castle resisted until he knew more about the picture. When Columbia said it was an A picture starring Jimmy

Stewart and Margaret Sullavan, Castle was thrilled. His new wife, however, was not. She cabled back that is was too late to leave because all the
flights were booked, but Cohn replied that he had already arranged the
air travel and the pair was to leave July 1. It's possible Cohn's only reason for promising a honeymoon for Castle and his wife was to get him
to do the filming. Once accomplished he had no reason to keep the
director on a paid holiday and asked him to return.

When Ellen and Bill arrived in New York they decided to rest the
night before flying to Hollywood, but that evening Bill was awakened by
a sharp pain in his abdomen. Thinking it might be his appendix, Castle
was to go to the hospital, but the hotel doctor diagnosed his illness as a
kidney stone, and Castle rested at the hotel until the next afternoon
when the stone finally passed.

Castle headed back to Hollywood and found that his A picture starring Jimmy Stewart had been canceled. He probably wondered if the
film had ever actually existed to begin with.

Instead of moving onto A pictures, Cohn told Castle that William
Goetz and Leo Spitz had recently joined together to form a Universal-
International and they were looking for talented directors. Goetz
reportedly called Cohn and Castle's name came up. "I think I'd like to
try another studio, Harry…If it's ok with you," said Castle.

Again, it's important to note that Castle's contract with Columbia
actually ended in 1947 and some reports show his next contract with
the studio didn't appear until 1953. Besides *The Gentleman From
Nowhere, The Lady From Shanghai* was the only picture Castle made for
the studio between 1947 and 1953. Castle directed *Texas, Brooklyn and
Heaven* for United Artists, which was released in 1948. If the studio did
not renew his contract, Castle's claims of suspension were unfounded,
and it would have made sense for him to sign on with Universal when
the opportunity arose.

A New Studio to Call Home

It was 1949 when Castle moved over to Universal-International under a three-year contract that he claimed was double what Columbia was paying him. The fledgling studio was actually a series of bungalows that Bill Castle said looked something like "a country club" with "flowers and manicured lawns that gave the feeling of peace and tranquillity."

His first picture was entitled *Johnny Stool Pigeon*, a B-movie thriller starring Shelley Winters and a newcomer named Tony Curtis. The picture sank at the box office as did most of the other pictures the studio released in its early years. What followed was a series of low-budget mediocre B pictures that continued Castle's string of little-known and lesser-seen pictures—*Undertow* (1949), *It's a Small World* (1950), *The Fat Man* (1951), *Cave of Outlaws* (1951), and finally, *Hollywood Story* (1951).

In 1952 Universal-International wanted Castle to resign with the studio, but after a disappointing three years Castle went back to see Harry Cohn and Columbia. They offered him a chance to return to the studio he had called home for so long and promised him both more money and more pictures. He gladly accepted and signed another contract with the studio that would keep him there through 1956.

Back at Columbia Castle dove into projects, but the quality of the work had changed little. The studio was actually undergoing change as well during the 50s. Television was now the competition and B films were given even less attention and money than before. The studio embraced television, instead of fighting it, and developed a production arm specifically for the new device.

However, the studio was releasing far fewer films than it had in the past. While the studio reached its peak of releasing 59 films in 1950 and 63 films in 1951, 1953 saw only 47 films released and 1954 had only 35 in theaters. Financial problems also dogged the studio for the better part of the decade as profits grew slowly or not at all.

Serpent of the Nile, Conquest of Cochise, Slaves of Babylon, Fort Ti, Charge of the Lancers and *Jesse James vs. The Daltons* were all released in 1953 and directed by Castle, but none were A pictures. Castle had now become King of the Bs. In 1954 and 1955, little had changed, *Drums of Tahiti, Battle of Rogue River, Masterson of Kansas, The Iron Glove, The Law vs. Billy the Kid* and a number of others followed. Castle was even loaned out to RKO for *The Americano*, but the picture was still a B movie.

The Saracen Blade was the only important film Castle released in 1954 and it was important or personal reasons. Ricardo Montalban, who found later fame in television on *Fantasy Island*, starred in the 13th Century epic and he and his wife invited the Castles to their home for dinner to celebrate the end of production. Ellen Castle was pregnant at the time with their first child. She liked Ricardo Montalban's wife's name so much she asked if she could give the name to her child if it was a girl. The Montalbans were honored by the idea and surely enough, on October 2, 1954 Ellen Castle gave birth to a daughter which they named Georgiana.

Uranium Boom and *The Houston Story* were released in 1956 and Castle was ripe for change. The latter had been the last straw for Castle. It was a difficult film to make, with filming taking place in Texas during August. The unbearable heat took its toll on cast and crew. The star of the picture Lee J. Cobb was rushed to the hospital with pains in his chest in the middle of production and doctors said he'd need several months to recuperate from a heart attack. Three more days of location shooting were needed before heading back to Hollywood, so Castle cast himself in the role and performed the remainder of Lee's scenes. The two men looked alike and long shots were used so it looked like the same man.

Once back in Hollywood 10 weeks went by while Lee recovered and a week before he was due back on the picture he suffered another attack and the part had to be recast. Actor Gene Barry took over the role, but the studio wouldn't allow another location shoot so the earlier footage of both Cobb and Castle was needed to finish the film. In the end, all three men are in the picture as the same character.

Columbia was facing the same troubles all Hollywood studios were facing. The days when the studios ran Hollywood were coming to an end. Columbia recorded its first loss in the 1957/58 fiscal year. Harry Cohn had undergone an operation to fight cancer in 1954 and his health had been deteriorating since. Jack Cohn died in 1956 and the studio felt a great blow. In early 1958 Harry Cohn also died and the Columbia that Castle had grown up with wasn't the same, but by that point Castle was heading in a new direction.

With his contract at Columbia ended, Castle took a break from the grind, and was the producer of a syndicated TV anthology series called *Men of Annapolis* in 1957. During the time off he began thinking about his next move. He wanted more and began looking for a project of his own and to step into the role of an independent producer. "I wanted to work for myself," he was quoted as saying at the time. "But I had to find something sure."

II

The Fright Years

Death by Fright

In 1951, Alfred A. Knopf's publishing house published a book entitled *The Marble Forest* by Theo Durant. Promotion of the novel described it with these lines: "How long could a four-year-old girl live buried in a casket. The man on the phone had said five hours, maybe six, and then, with a choked-back laugh, hung up."

The book was not the standard fare for a publishing house like Knopf, which was best known for prestigious literary works. But since prestigious literary works were rarely big sellers the publisher also printed more commercial works to pay for its work with higher literary aspirations. *The Marble Forest* was most definitely a commercial work.

Unaware of the book, it was several years later when William Castle and his wife headed out for an evening at the movies, deciding to take in Henri-Georges Clouzot's thriller *Diabolique*. Released in 1955, the French thriller eventually made its way to the United States where it was met with much anticipation. The thriller was a huge critical and financial success, all the more amazing because it was a foreign film with subtitles. Theaters were packed and lines formed outside of mostly young teen-age patrons waiting to see this frightening new film. Promotion for the film asked moviegoers not to give away the ending to others and for theaters not to admit viewers once the film had started.

William Castle had heard all the commotion and wanted to see what all the fuss was about. "Word was out that *Diabolique* was doing great business, but I never expected the excitement that surrounded the theater," Castle recalled later. "It was an amazing phenomenon," he wrote. "hundreds of youngsters waiting patiently to have the shit scared out of them."

It reportedly took Castle and his wife several days before they actually got into the theater to see the show, but when they did, they were not disappointed.

An Idea Is Born

Castle loved the film. He felt "transfixed" as the movie unfolded before him. His wife, who ironically hated horror movies, wanted to leave, but he urged her to stay as a dead body emerged from the tub and the theater erupted in screams.

After the film Castle could not get *Diabolique* and its fans out of his mind. He saw an opportunity. If a foreign horror film with subtitles could generate that much success, Castle was sure an American version would do even better. And he wanted to be the one to make it. "I decided then and there that I had a wide open chance at something special. If a foreign horror picture could draw such a huge crowd, think what an all-English-speaking picture would do!" he wrote.

It had been roughly five years since *The Marble Forest* had first been published. Castle began looking for his *Diabolique* immediately after seeing the film. He read novels, screenplays, stage plays and more in search of a story with the same horrific elements of the Clouzot classic. He believed he found it when he happened upon *The Marble Forest*. Castle asked his wife to read the book and when she agreed he decided this was the story for him.

When he checked into the purchasing the movie rights to the book he found that the author, Theo Durant, was actually the pen name of a San Francisco mystery writers club. Twelve well-known mystery writers each wrote a chapter to the book and an editor compiled the completed work by adjusting the styles so it read like the work of a single author.

Castle easily acquired the rights for what he called "a modest price plus a small percentage of the film."

Castle contacted Robb White, a screenwriter and novelist with whom he had worked with in the 1957 series *Men of Annapolis*, and asked him if he'd like to join forces and write the screenplay which Castle would then direct. White agreed.

Newspaper ads for 'Macabre' promoted the life insurance policy against death by fright.

The Horrific Story

The story is centered in a small town where the town doctor's three-year-old daughter—a year younger than in the book—turns up missing. Starring William Prince as the doctor, the movie begins at a funeral home where the owner is reporting to the town sheriff, played by Jim Backus, that someone broke into his mortuary and stole a child's coffin.

A short time later the doctor returns home where he and his house-keeper/nanny, played by veteran actress Ellen Corby, find his daughter has disappeared. When the doctor ventures out to find her the phone rings and the doctor's nurse, Polly, who has returned with him, answers to hear a man tell her he has kidnapped the daughter. The girl has been buried her alive, giving her four or five hours to live—not the five or six described in the book.

The doctor, who believes everyone in town blames him for the deaths of several prominent people including his own wife who died in child-birth because he wasn't there, feels the police will do nothing to help him and heads off, only with the help of Polly, to find his daughter. The two head to the cemetery after finding the little girl's teddy bear left on the doorstep with fresh dirt on it. They look for a fresh grave where the girl might be buried, but fresh dirt has been scattered on many of the plots and the pair fear they won't find the right one in time.

Coincidentally, the evening of the kidnapping is also the evening of a funeral for the little girl's blind aunt who has recently died and the doctor is blamed for being unable to save her from a botched abortion. The night funeral is planned because the blind woman lived her life in darkness and it's therefore decided she should be laid to rest in darkness. The doctor's father-in-law, who is the dead woman's father and the missing girl's grand-father, is shaken by the news of the kidnapping and fears her death will be too much for him after already having lost both his daughters.

The story unfolds as the key characters gather for the funeral and search for the missing girl. The film reaches its surprising climax, after a several deaths and shocks, when a coffin is opened to reveal a gruesome mummy of a small girl and the grandfather suffers a fatal heart attack, falling into the freshly dug grave for his daughter.

As rain pours down a gun emerges from a sea of umbrellas and the doctor is shot. It is then revealed that the doctor planned the entire hoax to scare his father-in-law to death, so he would inherit the man's $10 million estate and blackmailed the funeral home owner, who has shot him, into assisting him with the hoax. The doctor is taken to his medical offices and dies shortly after and his nurse finds a key in his hand that unlocks the door to his office where his young daughter has been sleeping through the entire picture.

Once the screenplay was crafted, Castle and White decided a name change was in order. "Robb, the title *The Marble Forest* is wrong for the picture," said Castle.

"Why, it's a good title," responded White.

"It's not box office," said Castle. "We need something that will pull customers in."

"How about *Buried Alive*?" suggested White.

"Not bad," he answered. "But I'd prefer a one-word title."

Ghastly was suggested, then *Gruesome,* but Castle was surely still thinking along the lines of the French hit *Diabolique* when he suggested *Macabre*, a French term for the dance of death. In addition to the name, the film had many similarities to *Diabolique*, including the plot twist at the end and the theme of trying to shock someone to death who had a heart condition.

Castle reportedly approached his old studio, Columbia, with his screenplay in hopes of getting them to bankroll the picture. Sam Briskin, who took over as head of the studio following Harry Cohn's death, turned down Castle's offer. Castle said that the studio was amiable to the idea, and to his request to direct the picture, but would not agree to let him produce the film because he had never produced a full-length motion picture before. "There's a big difference between producing and directing," Briskin reportedly told Castle. "Columbia will let you direct anytime, but we cannot take a chance on you producing."

Frustrated with his inability to get financing, Castle discussed the option of financing the picture with his wife. "Ellen and I dined at an expensive restaurant that evening, and over the chocolate soufflé, I took the plunge. 'Darling, I've got a wonderful idea,' " he said.

"I know. You want to mortgage our house and go into business for yourself. It's about time!" she replied.

Castle proposed the opportunity to White, who agreed to help fund the venture, and then Castle refinanced his home and set forth on creating his own *Diabolique*. Together the men invested $90,000 to make the film.

Because of the limited budget, no stars would be asked to star in the picture, the closest actor to celebrity status was Jim Backus. Backus, who would later go onto fame and fortune as Thurston Howell in *Gilligan's Island* several years later, had a long list of credits to his name. His biggest success to date was his portrayal as James Dean's father in the hit *Rebel Without A Cause*. In addition to Backus, Prince and Corby, the cast included Christine White, Jacqueline Scott and Susan Morrow.

Castle's memoirs claim that production on the film began on August 15, 1958, but this is impossible since the film was released in July that year—one month before production supposedly began. It's probable that Castle was confused on the year and production actually began on August 15, 1957 instead. This seems more logical, because filming lasted only for nine days and post-production would have carried Castle through the fall with a first cut of the film ready that winter. Castle then would have had time to arrange his insurance policy gimmick and start searching for a distributor in the early months of 1958. If the film was sold by spring 1958, the distributor could then have prepared the prints and advertising and released the picture that summer.

This scenario seems appropriate, except that Harry Cohn was still leading Columbia until his death in early 1958, which means Castle's meeting with Sam Briskin may have been another of Castle's tales.

However, in Castle's defense, it is possible that Briskin would have been in the position to turn Castle down in 1957, as he was a high level executive with the studio at the time. Although, it is also possible that Castle approached Columbia in early 1958 about distributing the film and it was in this meeting that Briskin turned Castle down. Nonetheless, production must have taken place in 1957.

Location shooting took place in Chino, California, which became the small town of Thornton in the film. Some additional interior shots, including the cemetery footage, were filmed on the soundstages of Hollywood. Cinematographer Carl Guthrie, who Castle had worked with several years earlier on his film *The Hollywood Story*, was asked to handle the cinematography.

Castle believed he was "getting a masterpiece—another *Diabolique*—only better," but after viewing a rough cut of the finished picture he admitted to himself that "something was missing."

White suggested they add more horror, but Castle said that would not be possible because they were out of money. "It doesn't have that blood-curdling quality I tried to get," he said disappointingly.

A Gimmick 'Insures' Success

In his memoirs, Castle recalled that while lying in bed one night, concerned about the success of his first independently produced and directed film, he came up with a brainstorm for ensuring success. "My house was mortgaged to the hilt and I would probably have to sell the goddamn bed. The same nagging thought kept me awake—something was missing. But what? Suddenly, sitting bolt upright, I shouted, 'Wake up, Ellen—I've got it! An insurance policy!'"

"Go back to sleep…We've already got an insurance policy," replied his wife.

Castle believe that with the proper gimmick patrons would line up to see his horrific feature. Insuring the moviegoers against death by fright seemed like the perfect ploy. Castle knew that Lloyds of London claimed they would insure anything, so he contacted them the next morning and told them he wanted to insure everyone in the world. He said in his memoirs that they abruptly hung up on him.

Castle then made an appointment with their brokers in the U.S. and went in person to explain his idea. Castle explained to the agents that the policy was only a gimmick for his movie, but that he wanted to insure the world, or at least the people who went to see his movie. The agents told him it was not possible, but then decided what they could do would be to insure Castle himself against any claims from the audience.

A policy was devised that if any claim did come forth, Castle would collect $1,000, which he would then pay to the beneficiary. Since such a policy had never been written it was difficult to come up with a cost for it. The insurance agents asked Castle how many people he thought might die while watching his motion picture. "Nobody's going to drop dead," promised Castle. "It's just a publicity stunt."

The men then began to bargain for a proper rate to the policy. First, it was suggested that 25 people might die, then they offered 20. Castle said two and the agents said ten. Finally, it was agreed that five people could conceivably die of fright during the film. At $1,000 per beneficiary, the rate of the policy was set at $5,000. Castle, already in debt from making the movie, agreed to pay the policy off in installments over a period of two years.

Now that he had his finished picture and his gimmick to make it a success, Castle set forth on selling the movie to a distributor and getting it into theaters. He approached Warner Bros. who agreed to see the picture.

After viewing the finished film and hearing his sales gimmick, they offered him $45,000 and 25 percent of the profits. "But I paid $90,000, sir. I'll be losing money," responded Castle.

"We decided it's a risk picture," said the Warner's executive. "And with our paying for the prints and advertising…you must be willing to take the gamble."

Castle said no.

Several weeks later, Castle claimed in his memoirs, that a Warner Bros. publicity man stole his insurance policy gimmick on a new picture at the studio. When Castle found out he threatened to sue. Warners supposedly pulled the gimmick and fired the publicity man when they found out what had happened. And to make it up to Castle they offered to buy the picture for the entire $90,000 it cost to make. Again, Castle refused, but dropped his suit against the studio. He believed he could get a better deal.

Castle next contacted Allied Artists, a young studio known for its cheap, low-budget features. "They need pictures," thought Castle.

Allied Artists offered Castle $150,000 and 75 percent of the profits. He took it.

MACABRE

The Producers of the film MACABRE, undertake to pay the sum of ONE THOUSAND DOLLARS in the event of the death by fright of any member of the audience during the performance.

BENEFICIARY AGREEMENT

In the event of my decease by fright during the performance of the motion picture "MACABRE", I hereby instruct the producers to pay ONE THOUSAND DOLLARS ($1,000) Life Benefit to my beneficiary named below.

BENEFICIARY'S NAME   RELATIONSHIP

I understand that if I have a known heart or nervous condition the One Thousand Dollars ($1,000) is not payable.

NAME

The above agreement is insured by Lloyd's of London.

A copy of the actual insurance policy moviegoers received during the showing of 'Macabre.'

The Release

Macabre premiered in New York on July 23, 1958 as the lead picture of a double bill with another Allied Artists film called *Hell's Five Hours*. Insurance policies against death by fright were given out to all the patrons in attendance and larger versions were hung outside many of the theaters to promote the movie. The policy was also used in the advertisements.

As the film begins a clock is shown on the screen and a narrator instructs filmgoers that each has been insured for the 115 minute-long feature against death by fright. Lloyds of London was cautious enough to exclude anyone with pre-existing heart conditions or those considering suicide.

Castle promoted the gimmick almost as much as the film itself. In interviews and articles he claimed he actually flew to London to arrange the policy and in promotion materials sent to theaters he strongly urged theater owners to play up the insurance policy angle. In publicity kits, a series of promotions with severed heads, funeral processions, corpses and graves were used. Promotional text read, "If it frightens you to death—you'll be buried free of charge," See it with someone who can carry you home." and "We hung the cameraman to keep him from disclosing the terrifying surprises."

The gimmick worked like a charm. *Variety* reported that total distribution of insurance policies topped 10 million. No claims were ever filed, but patrons did line up to see what was so scary they might die of fright while watching.

Castle attended openings in many major cities to promote the film. In Boston, he said long lines formed outside with people clutching their policies in anticipation of the film, and in Philadelphia he said the film broke the house record for attendance at one theater. Castle then began catering to the excitement by having uniformed nurses in the theater lobbies in case patrons were in need of medical assistance.

For the premiere in Minneapolis, Castle rented a black hearse, similar to the one a cartoon caricature of him is seen driving across the screen as the credits roll at the end of the picture. He then rented a coffin to make a horrific entrance.

"Covered in a dark cape and hidden from the lines of people, I got inside the coffin and closed the lid. It was pitch black and I had trouble breathing," he remembered years later.

Castle went on to say that attendants took the coffin from the hearse and placed it on the sidewalk so he could make his grand entrance, but when he went to open the lid it was stuck and he couldn't get out. He said he knocked himself out, banging and screaming for help, and ended up lying on the sidewalk with smelling salts being used on him to wake him up.

Later, he said one theatergoer accosted him outside the theater, complaining, "You're the producer of this picture, aren't you, mister?...It's not horrific—it's horrible."

Those sentiments were not uncommon after the picture's release. While patrons flocked to the theater, many were disappointed to find the film wasn't as frightening as expected. Castle's gimmick itself had drawn people in, but had also lifted their expectations to a level Castle couldn't meet. "I had no cast and no money so I had to do something else to compel the audience to come into the theater," Castle reportedly said. "Not having stars or a high budget I had to do something different and I became, in effect, the king of the gimmicks."

But even with the gimmicks, or perhaps because of, the critics were not kind. *The New York Times* wrote: "Chances of any heirs and assigns' collecting on the proffered $1,000 policies seem slim, judging by the goings-on in this somber but tepid shocker...Although their midnight meandering generates some goose-pimples, it is all the more foggy than frightening. There is a fairly surprising switch at the climax, a cute set of credit titles and four cadavers. All of this can be taken without a physician in attendance."

In the end, however, Castle had succeeded. His film, complete with insurance gimmick, had pulled in approximately $5 million in box-office receipts. It's important to note that while *Macabre* was not a leading box office draw in 1958 and many other pictures outshined the horror tale, it was an astounding success considering the film cost a mere $90,000 to make. By comparison, Alfred Hitchcock set forth in 1959 to make his own low-budget shocker to capitalize on the success of films like *Diabolique* and *Macabre*. Hitchcock's *Psycho* easily outpunched *Macabre* at the box office, taking in more than $9 million in its initial release in 1960. But the film cost more than $850,000 to make and received far greater publicity and promotion than Castle could have ever achieved.

With his success, William Castle was in business and the profits would be poured into his next frightful film and an equally hair-raising gimmick.

A Haunting We Will Go

With his financial status as an independent filmmaker on solid ground from the success of *Macabre*, Castle knew he had at last found a niche he could fill. And Allied Artists was pleased enough with the first venture to ask Castle to quickly produce a new horror picture to follow on the heels of *Macabre*. Castle was only too happy to oblige.

The easiest route to take was to go with the tried and true. Castle and screenwriter Robb White decided an old fashioned haunted house would do the trick and it had worked in the past with many horror classics capitalizing on dark dreary castles, cob webs and things that go bump in the night. Most recently, Abbott and Costello had been finding success in a string of haunted features, including *Abbott and Costello Meet the Mummy* and *Abbott and Costello Meet Dr. Jekyll and Mr. Hyde*. Now it was Castle's turn.

House on Haunted Hill

House on Haunted Hill quickly took form as the tale of a deadly old home rented by a wealthy man who offers $10,000 to any of his party guests who agree to spend the night there and survive. White once again penned the script, along with the help of Castle, and both men joined in the financial venture to follow their first hit. Soon the director was looking for a lead actor who he felt was elegant but had an offbeat personality to make the picture work.

One evening, while drinking coffee in a small coffee shop near a Hollywood studio, Castle spotted Vincent Price sitting alone at one of the other tables. Castle wrote in his memoirs that he had met Price backstage at a play a number of years earlier, but when he reintroduced himself to the actor, Price didn't remember him. Even so, Castle asked if he could join him and Price agreed.

During their conversation that evening Price admitted to Castle that he was depressed because he had just lost out on a part he wanted very much. Hearing this sad news, Castle launched into his pitch to convince Price to star in his new picture.

Contrary to what Castle says in his memoirs, working with William Castle never opened up a "whole new career" for Vincent Price—it was a career he had already been well established in. Working with Castle only helped to reinforce his role as a horror star. In 1939 Price starred in *Tower of London* and soon after found himself cast in a wide range of horror films. *The Invisible Man Returns, Shock, Abbott and Costello Meet the Ghosts*, and *House of Wax* were a few of the more memorable titles. And although Price starred in several non-horror classics, including *Laura* and *The Song of Bernadette,* his 1953 film *House of Wax* in 3-D became the highest grossing horror film of the time and solidified Price's place in the genre.

In addition to *House on Haunted Hill*, Price also acted in several other horror films between 1958 and 1959, making it somewhat of a watershed year for the horror star. *The Bat, The Fly, Return of the Fly* and another Castle picture, *The Tingler,* ensconced Price in the genre and made it nearly impossible for him to escape.

But in 1958 the opportunity spelled steady work for the actor and Price decided to hear Castle out. "I'm starting a picture in a few weeks," Castle explained…"A millionaire invites six people to spend the night in a haunted house. He chooses the people carefully and offers to pay a great deal of money to each one if they agree to spend the entire night in the haunted house."

'House on Haunted Hill' promoted Castle's second gimmick, Emergo, where a skeleton emerged from behind movie screens to frighten viewers at the appropriate time.

"Sounds interesting, go on," responded Price.

"During the night, many strange ghostly things happen...blood dripping from the ceiling...walls shaking...apparitions appearing. The millionaire—the part I want you to play—has plotted to kill his wife. She plots to kill you...It's a battle of wits."

"Who wins?" asked Price.

"You do, of course. She tries to throw you into a vat of boiling acid."

"How charming," answered the actor in his droll style.

"Suddenly you rise slowly from the vat of acid...body eaten away. You're just bones—a living skeleton! Your skeleton scares the shit out of your wife and she loses her balance and falls into the vat of acid," Castle continued.

"Delicious...Where the hell am I?" asked Price.

"You're working your phony skeleton, like a puppeteer.

Castle explained the rest of the picture and Price was on board.

The Production

In addition to Price, the cast called for five party guests, a pair of servants, and a beautiful but devilish wife capable of murder. And although Castle had succeeded with *Macabre* and his budget for *House on Haunted Hill* could stretch beyond $90,000, and was budgeted at $150,000, he still needed to keep expenses down and couldn't afford stars in the film.

Richard Long, Alan Marshal, Carolyn Craig, Elisha Cook Jr., Julie Mitchum, Leona Anderson, and Howard Hoffman filled the roles of the dinner guests and servants, but Castle needed just the right actress for the role of the sixth party guest, Vincent Price's wife.

Carol Ohmart was a former Miss Utah who placed fourth in the Miss America Pageant in 1946. After carving out a successful modeling career she was discovered by Paramount Pictures. In 1955, being groomed as the studio's answer to Marilyn Monroe, she was signed to a seven-year contract and a $2 million publicity campaign was launched to notify the world. But Ohmart's career never took off.

Billboards and ads in Hollywood trade papers announced her and fan magazines began talking about her as the next big star. Her first picture, *The Scarlet Hour*, was directed by *Casablanca* director Michael Curtiz would unveil her to the world in VistaVision. But the film earned only mediocre reviews and Ohmart's unsympathetic character did nothing to endear her to the audience. Her star was already fading and her career had only just begun. She made a few more minor films that did nothing to help her career and by 1958 her fan club was out of business and little work was coming her way. But William Castle felt she would provide the right image for the murderous wife of Vincent Price's Frederick Loren. And, besides Price, she was the closest thing to a star he could afford. Ohmart was hired for role of Annabelle Loren.

Production quickly got underway and Castle again used the talents of Carl Guthrie for the cinematography. Von Dexter, who would go on to score several other Castle pictures, was hired to produce the music which aptly used moans, chains and a variety of other sounds, to produce a haunting score that captured the feel of the film perfectly. The house used in the film was actually a Frank Lloyd Wright home built entirely of concrete overlooking Los Angeles. While not a typical haunted house, it did have an ominous presence for the opening scenes of the picture.

The Horrific Tale

The movie starts with a black screen and only the sounds of chains and screams are heard. Moments later the head of Elisha Cook appears and sets the stage by saying, "The ghosts are moving tonight...restless...hungry. May I introduce myself? I'm Watson Pritchard. In just a minute I'll show you the only really haunted house in the world. Since it was built, more than a century ago, seven people, including my brother, have been murdered in it. Since then I've owned the house. I've only spent one night there and when they found me in the morning I was almost dead."

Vincent Price next appears on screen to say he is Frederick Loren and has rented the house on haunted hill, inviting patrons to join him for the night. The guests begin arriving and soon the fun begins. A test pilot, newspaper columnist, secretary, psychiatrist and the house's owner have each been invited to join Loren and his wife for the evening.

Each guest is in need of money and is promised the pay of $10,000 if they survive the night. If they do not survive, their beneficiary gets the cash and if Loren is the one to die, his estate has been instructed to pay. The party guests are then each given a party favor, which is actually a miniature coffin with a loaded gun inside.

The film then travels throughout the house offering occasional scares and plot twists until the screaming end when Ohmart's character meets her doom in the cellar, falling into the vat of acid following the shock of seeing her husband's living skeleton emerge from it.

In many ways, *House on Haunted Hill* is the quintessential William Castle horror picture. All the elements work together to provide the moody horrific film he was looking for and teen-agers were delighted at the chance to see severed heads, a hanging, several ghouls and the climactic finale. But Castle wanted to give them something more. He needed another gimmick. He said the audience began to expect it of him and after the success of *Macabre*, theater owners asked him for another stunt.

As a follow up on his nurses in the theater lobby gimmick, this time Castle devised a "You must have your blood pressure taken in the lobby before viewing this film" area. But that wasn't enough, so he came up with something more.

Previews for the film were set up to test audience reaction and Castle claimed the first test didn't work because the audience was wrong. "There were no young people in the theater," Castle explained.

One elderly man, who was sitting next to Castle before he got up and left, told the director, "This is the biggest piece of shit I've ever seen."

But when the film was tested again, Castle said he made sure there were plenty of teen-agers in the crowd and the audience response was enthusiastic.

Time for Another Gimmick

Allied Artists met with Castle to discuss his ideas for another gimmick, but one had not been developed yet. Ghostly sound effects were suggested and managed to find their way into the film. Then, someone suggested dressing the ushers as ghosts, but Castle passed on the idea as inferior. Then he decided on Emergo.

Emergo was Castle's name for having a skeleton march from the screen into the theater. Towards the end of the picture Vincent Price is maneuvering his skeleton across the screen as he scares his poor wife to death. At one point the skeleton reaches the end of the screen and leaves the picture. Castle devised that at that moment a life-size skeleton would emerge from a box next to the screen and be carried by cables out over the audience. Moments later it would return to its resting place and back to Price's hands on the big screen.

"We'll have to manufacture hundreds of 12-foot skeletons and to install them in the theater will cost a fortune," said Steve Broidy, an executive with Allied Artists.

"The theaters will pay for them," Castle promised. "I've even got a name for my gimmick—Emergo!"

Castle used an engineer Herman Townsley to craft the device that would carry the skeleton out from beside the screen and over the audience and then back again. Promotion for the new process hinted that the gimmick "hurls flying objects throughout the theater auditorium," and that "the terror zooms right out at you."

The Release

The film premiered in New York on March 11, 1959 and again *The New York Times* was not pleased. Reviewer Howard Thompson wrote that a "load of junk from Allied Artists was unveiled to the public." Of the gimmick, he added, "This bore also introduces 'the amazing new wonder, Emergo.' What is it? Not much of anything. As a skeleton entered the proceedings yesterday," the reviewer wrote "…the house lights of the 58th Street Theatre dimmed and a luminescent counterpart appeared suspended next to the screen. With a whistling of wires, and considerable audience snickering, it slid straight forward to the balcony, blankly eyed the first-row customers, and slid back."

Thompson concluded the review by adding that the skeleton "was one performer who obviously couldn't wait to meet the public and instantly regretted it."

But once again, even with lousy reviews the film succeeded. When it premiered in San Francisco, Castle claimed, it took the theater three shows before they got the skeleton working right. But when they did they were not disappointed. Castle recalled in his memoirs that "Thousands of kids had been waiting on line for hours for the evening performances. That line was six blocks long!" he added that the theater was completely sold out.

In reality, not all theaters were given 12-foot plastic skeletons. Director John Landis recalled seeing the film to one interviewer, saying, "[I]t was the tackiest thing. It was a paper skeleton on a string that came out over the audience."

It's likely that most theaters started with the real thing and ended up with the paper lookalike, because as director Joe Dante recalled, "There were apparently very few theaters in which the skeleton survived, because once the kids found out that it was happening, they would come back with slingshots and popcorn boxes. That was a pretty expensive gimmick."

In the end it paid off. The film pulled in $2 million in its first few months of release and some reports put the film's total gross at $6 million by the end of its release. Castle and White were already at work on their next feature. And so pleased were they with their leading man that, once again, Vincent Price was on hand as their star. And Castle's biggest gimmick was just around the corner.

Time for a Tingler

By the late 1950s horror films were all the rage in Hollywood and in theaters across the country. Perhaps it was the cold war, the threat of total destruction from nuclear war, or what others called the effects of suburban isolation and alienation. Whatever the cause, horror films offered a face to the fear—something tangible and something we could wage war on and conquer in less than two hours.

In 1957, 52 horror pictures graced the big screen. In 1958, there were 75, including William Castle's *Macabre*. In 1959, 100 horrors were planned for the big screen, including *House on Haunted Hill* and Castle's follow-up feature, *The Tingler*. In 1959, *Playboy* predicted that one-third of all the films created in Hollywood would be horrors, costing approximately $10 million to make and raking in $100 million at the box office. Castle only wanted his share of the profits.

What Next?

The success of *Macabre* not only provided William Castle with the funds and the clout to move ahead with production of *House on Haunted Hill*, it also enabled him to produce and begin another horror picture before *Haunted Hill* was even in theaters. And it carried him back to the studio he once called home—Columbia Pictures.

It must have been a victorious moment for William Castle. As a contract employee, Castle started at the bottom of the ladder, taking step after step, always hoping to reach the top of the ladder. He became trapped in the middle, directing B picture after B picture, and never saw the fruits of his labor result in his directing a major motion picture with the studio.

Now, after more than 15 years of towing the studio line, Castle stepped out on his own, risking his career on a shot at something better. And even though the pictures were still not garnering the acclaim he longed for, at least they were making money—and plenty of it. And, in the end, that's why the studios were in business. Columbia now wanted independent producer-director William Castle to make a picture for the studio.

Back Home

Back at Columbia, he was now set up in his own production company. He had hired Dona Holloway, one of Harry Cohn's former executive secretaries, to be his associate producer and again took advantage of Robb White's talents to craft the script for *The Tingler*. In addition to his prolific career, Castle's home front also expanded when his wife gave birth to their second child in December 1958—Terry Castle.

If *House on Haunted Hill* was Castle's quintessential camp horror picture, then *The Tingler* was the film that provided him with his ultimate promotion.

It was familiar territory for Castle by now. Once again, Vincent Price was back at the helm as the leading star. White's script had the same elements that made the other films work at the box office—some blood, murder plots, a few dead bodies and a shocking twist at the end. In other words, it had all the elements of success.

For the first time, William Castle stepped before his audience on film. His ego had been boosted by his success and now he wanted to take credit for his work and let the public know who he was. Opening up *The Tingler,* he introduced himself as the director of the picture and offered these words, "Don't be embarrassed about opening your mouth and letting rip with all you've got," he said. "Because the person in the seat right next to you will probably be screaming too. And remember, a scream at the right time may save your life."

It was an important step for Castle. He had longed for success and to make his mark. And although his films had received poor treatment at the hands of the critics, moviegoers embraced his flair and showmanship making his features successful. It was those fans he wanted to reach. And it was about this time that he helped launch his own fan club. Teenagers soon took over and the fan clubs were cropping up across the country.

Castle wanted the acclaim of success and had already appeared before the camera in several films in his early years with Columbia, usually as an extra without any lines. He had also strongly admired two other major directors who had stepped before the cameras. Orson Welles' performances on screen had made him a celebrity as well as a director and Castle wanted to achieve the same status.

But more than Welles, it was Alfred Hitchcock who had influenced him. Hitchcock had been making cameo appearances in his films for years, and when his TV series debuted, Hitchcock appeared before each show introducing the story with his dry and dark humor. Castle took the same approach, but while Hitchcock came off more elusive, Castle became much more approachable and good humored. He became a ham before the cameras knowing it was all in good fun and no one would take it seriously.

It was an important move for William Castle. For at this time he had become confident enough in what he was doing to stand up and accept responsibility for it. While reviewers continued to pan the director's efforts, the public came out in droves to see what he would come up with next. He appeared before them and tried to establish a relationship with what was mostly a younger generation of moviegoers.

Vincent Price would star in two of Castle's most famous films, 'House on Haunted Hill' and 'The Tingler,' both released in 1959.

The Horrific Tale

When the story begins we find that Price portrays Dr. Warren Chapin, a doctor/coroner who is studying the effects fright has on the body. As a coroner he performs autopsies on criminals who meet their end in the electric chair and as a scientist he uses cats and dogs to study fear on the living. Price's character theorizes that fear generates a living creature within our bodies that lives in our spinal column. By screaming we make the creature powerless. If we do not, or cannot, scream the "Tingler," as he calls it, grows inside us, cracking our spine and killing us.

Chapin meets a man named Oliver "Ollie" Higgins who happens to be the brother-in-law of a man the coroner is working on. Ollie asks him for a ride into town and then invites Chapin into his home for coffee. During the visit, Chapin meets Ollie's wife Martha, a deaf mute who runs the movie theater below their home. When Chapin cuts himself Martha's fear of blood causes her body to tense up and then she passes out from shock.

Needing a patient, or guinea pig, to capture the "Tingler," Chapin believes the mute woman who cannot scream her fear away would be a perfect study. After she dies of fright, her husband allows the doctor to extract the "Tingler" from her body and with his hypothesis substantiated, he plans to offer his discovery to the world. Dr. Chapin places the beast in a small carrying case and returns to his home. The "Tingler," which looks something like a cross between a centipede and a lobster, is set free by the doctor's wife, who wants to kill him, and after a near-death experience, the doctor decides to return the "Tingler" to the dead woman's body and keep the evil from the world.

The doctor returns to the woman's home, which happens to be above a movie theater, and it's there that the "Tingler" escapes. Once loose the "Tingler" crawls through the floorboards to the projection room in the theater below. Moviegoers in the theater are watching the silent classic *Tol'able David*, but the film breaks and the screen goes white and then the film within the film become one when the creature slithers across the white screen and into the theater. The screen goes black and viewers hear Price announcing the "Tingler" is loose in the theater and moviegoers should scream for their lives.

In the end the doctor does return the "Tingler" to the body and rids the world of its evil. But the film offers one last shock when the "Tingler" causes the dead woman to sit up straight, shocking her husband, possibly to death, serving him justice as he was the one who scared her to death in the first place. In addition to Price, the cast included Judith Evelyn, the actress who plays the deaf mute. She and Price had actually worked together approximately 20 years earlier on Broadway in a production called "Angel Street." The remaining cast included Philip Coolidge, Darryl Hickman, Patricia Cutts and Pamela Lincoln.

The Terrifying Beast

Castle described his idea for the creature to artists at Columbia who then designed the beast. "Sort of like a lobster, but flat, and instead of claws it has long, slimy feelers," Castle explained. "That's what I think a 'Tingler' looks like."

In addition to what he hoped would be a terrifying beast and using himself to introduce the film, Castle tried several other new experiments with *The Tingler*. As usual, he shot the film in black and white, but decided to add color to one particular sequence, giving viewers a jolt.

Before the mute woman dies, her husband has an elaborate set-up to frighten her to death. When she steps into the bathroom she finds the faucet dripping with blood, which shocks us with the vivid red on a black and white screen and then she looks to the tub to find it full of oozing red blood. When an arm begins to emerge from the blood she is frightened to death. Her death certificate, pinned to the medicine cabinet door, lists the cause as death by "fright."

The blood bath was again a not-so-gentle lifting of an idea from *Diabolique*, and the early moments of the picture mirror *House on Haunted Hill* with screaming heads on a black screen.

This use of color in the black and white film was effective, but more shocking is the scene when Price uses LSD to study the effects of fear on himself. *The Tingler* is the first movie to acknowledge LSD, the mind-altering drug that would become popular among the youth drug craze approximately seven years later. It was the first time a major motion picture character "drops acid." In the scene, Price's character trips out on LSD while studying the effects of fear on himself.

A Shocking Gimmick

By now Castle was known as the King of Gimmicks and theater owners were expecting something to top his last two efforts. He claimed in his memoirs that his idea came one evening when he was at home reading in bed one night when the light on the night stand went out. He went into the kitchen, got a new bulb, and began to replace the light bulb when he got an electrical jolt because something was wrong with the wire to the lamp. "Suddenly I had my gimmick for *The Tingler*," he remembered.

He woke his wife up telling her his latest idea. "I'm going to buzz the asses of everyone in America by installing little motors under the seats of every theater in the country. When the 'Tingler' appears on the screen, the projectionist will push a button...The audiences will get a shock on their butts—and think the 'Tingler' is loose in the theater!"

He said his wife told him he was "stark raving mad."

At Columbia Studios he managed to convince the studio the effort would be worth the result. The studio designed the small boxes and deployed teams to travel throughout the country to install the equipment. A manual was printed giving diagrams and instructions for setting the device up to work correctly. The buzzers were attached to a relay that made its way into the projectionist's booth so that at just the right moments the shocks could be delivered.

Associate Producer Dona Holloway was credited with coming up with the name for the gimmick—Percepto, and soon promotion for the film promised the horror would be delivered with the new twist. Hollywood had been promising new viewing experiences for several years with concepts like 3-D, CinemaScope, VistaVision and more. Castle simply took the concept to a new level.

A week before the movie opened in Boston, Castle claimed a bored projectionist decided to test the equipment out on an audience watching *The Nun's Story*, starring Audrey Hepburn and the mostly female audience was jolted from the seats by the shocks. The gimmick worked and made its way throughout the country.

In another interview, screenwriter Robb White said *The Nun's Story* tale actually became a test of sorts to see if the gimmick actually worked before they moved ahead with the stunt. "We didn't want to buy thousands of vibrators without knowing whether they would really work out, so we scouted around until we found a theater in the Valley that was running *The Nun's Story*." The Audrey Hepburn drama was due to close Sunday evening with *The Tingler* opening on Monday. "We got in a huge crew of people to spend the day attaching the vibrators to the seats. But that night, just at the most tragic moments of *The Nun's Story,* somebody touched the master switch and the seats began vibrating in a wave after wave. There was absolute pandemonium!" said White.

Once again the gimmick succeeded and no longer were Castle's openings premieres, but were actually being called "screamieres." Castle was also known to plant actors in the audience to create havoc. One report claimed a woman in the audience was placed there by Castle and when Price told the audience the "Tingler" was loose in the theater she "burst into hysterics." She was then taken from the theater by a uniformed nurse.

The film earned mediocre to poor reviews, but the shocking seats pulled in millions of teen-agers. In the end Castle claimed he shocked as many at 20,000,000 behinds. The film reportedly earned as much as $6.5 million at the box office. And Vincent Price enjoyed the success of the film. "I was suddenly really in demand, but to play nasty chaps in movies calculated to frighten filmgoers out of their seats. I took to my new career with relish," said star Vincent Price.

The New York Times said the film could actually use a little gore. "For some time producer William Castle has been serving some of the worst, dullest little entries ever to snake into movie houses. This one, which he also directed, is about a rubbery-looking lobster…It failed to arouse the customer seated in the front of this viewer yesterday—a fearless lad who was sound asleep, snoring. Just keep us awake, Mr. Castle."

Not all showings were set up to buzz every moviegoers, though. By the time the film reached smaller suburban theaters only the occasional seat was wired for tingles. Filmmaker John Waters recalled that "By the time it got to my neighborhood theater, they only wired two or three of the seats. So I would get there early and find one of the seats that was rigged and sat there all day getting buzzed."

In a theater in Philadelphia it was reported that a truck driver, angered at shocks being delivered to his behind, ripped the seat out of its place to get to the device. It took five ushers to restrain him.

Castle's gimmicks worked because theater owners were happy to take part. Owners paid much of the cost associated with Castle's gimmicks and reaped the rewards with full houses of popcorn and candy-buying teen-agers eager to take part in the fun. Some houses began to get into the act themselves. In Seattle, one theater put airplane vomit bags at every seat in case viewers were shocked into sickness.

Theaters had been suffering as television began to cut in on their audience. Promising more became necessary for getting the public out of their living room and to the theater. Double features, gimmicks and the promise of bigger and better managed to keep the industry alive.

Now, all Castle had to do was to keep the ball rolling.

Thirteen Ghosts and Counting

By the dawn of a 1960s William Castle was most definitely on a roll. His first three films had packed the movie houses with teen-agers eager for a scare and grossed millions of dollars. For his follow-up to *The Tingler*, Castle decided on another ghost story, but unlike *House on Haunted Hill*, he wanted the ghosts to be the star of the picture, not Vincent Price.

In fact, it's important to note that while Castle has long been categorized as a B-movie director of mediocre talents, he never became a hack at his craft. His films are independent of one another and never fall into the same traps that many other directors found themselves falling into. Similar elements are found in Castle's pictures, but mainly because the genre of horror required those elements like ghosts and evil creatures, haunted houses and the occasional corpse.

In addition, his flair for gimmickry gave his audience the feeling that he genuinely enjoyed his new-found role. The gimmicks were unique, unprecedented and often went hand-in-hand with the film they touted.

His films also almost always offered a twist, so the climax was somewhat unexpected even though viewers knew it was coming. He and screenwriter Robb White strived for films that provided the public with what they expected, while trying to offer them the unexpected as well.

Macabre was followed by a completely different tale for *House on Haunted Hill*. And although Vincent Price returned for *The Tingler*, the story bares no resemblance to the earlier feature. His follow-up horror,

13 Ghosts would again be unlike his earlier films and the gimmick was developed with the movie in mind and built directly into the film.

Movie ads for '13 Ghosts' promoted Illusion-O as a new film process.

The Production

Once again Robb White teamed up with Castle to write the screenplay for the new ghost story. And Columbia was eager to take part as distributor of the film. And since Castle didn't like rehearsing actors, and claimed he never did so, the film was quickly put into production.

The story follows a typical American family that finds itself financially strapped until they inherit an old house from the father's recently-departed uncle. The family excitedly moves into the new home only to hear from the lawyer and housekeeper that the place is haunted. The family's eccentric old uncle Zorba had been experimenting with the afterlife before his mysterious death and developed a pair of goggles that were "ghost viewers" enabling the wearer to see the ghosts living in the house. The father is given the goggles along with the deed to the house and the story takes off when the ghosts begin to appear.

The family cannot sell the house because the will specifies they must live there or it goes to the state. And the catch to the story is that the uncle trusted no one in his last days and took all his money from his bank accounts and hid it somewhere in the house. In the end it is revealed the lawyer, Ben Rush, is trying to find the money before the family does and when the little boy discovers it hidden beneath the stairs, Rush tries to do away with him and take the money but the ghosts turn the tables and he gets done away with when he is crushed by a closing canopy bed, leaving the family with the money and the house.

The script appropriately called for 13 ghosts including: a clutching pair of hands; a floating head; a flaming skeleton; a screaming woman; a man with a meat cleaver, his unfaithful wife and the unfaithful wife's lover; an executioner with a severed head; a hanging woman; a lion and a lion tamer missing his head; Dr. Zorba, the dead uncle; and finally an unknown one.

Columbia was receptive to the idea and the film soon began production with the studio eager for a follow up to *The Tingler*. Theater owners were also looking forward to a follow-up film and a gimmick to draw the director's young fans.

The Gimmick—Illusion-O

Castle claimed that it took months for them to manage to get the ghosts to appear and disappear perfectly on film. They were the product of special effects that were to be added after the filming was finished. Actors performed as if they were seeing the apparitions when they were actually looking at nothing. The footage of the ghostly creatures were filmed separately and added in later in the editing process.

YOUR

13 GHOSTS

HORROR-SCOPE

To use this Horror-Scope properly, find out the exact hour within which you were born. Then consult the '13 Ghosts' to learn what lies ahead...for you!

SEE WILLIAM CASTLE'S

13 GHOSTS

in ILLUSION-O

A COLUMBIA PICTURES RELEASE

STATE THEATRE

Castle's 1960 film '13 Ghosts,' promoted Illusion-O as its gimmick. This time, moviegoers received glasses that allowed them to see the ghosts in the film.

To view the ghosts a pairs of glasses, similar to those used for 3-D, were manufactured and the process, following the success of Emergo and Percepto, was christened as "Illusion-O."

Eastmancolor was used to develop the process for including the ghosts in the film. While the feature was shot in black and white, the ghosts appeared in red and were shot on a blue background, so when viewers put on the blue and red tinted glasses the ghosts appeared. Subtitles were added to the finished film telling theatergoers when to use the viewer and when to remove it during the picture.

The Gimmick that Got Away

Castle wrote in his memoirs that during the a European tour to promote one of his earlier pictures he and his wife were taking a drive through the France countryside when they spotted an old boarded up house that look quite horrific. He came up with a fantastic idea of buying the house and having 20 million keys made, with one fitting the lock.

Castle initially decided he could use the gimmick, giving away a real haunted house, to promote his ghostly new motion picture. But Castle claimed that once the Illusion-O gimmick was developed he set the haunted house idea aside planning to use the gimmick on another picture. He never did.

Once again, it appears Castle wasn't exactly accurate in his memoirs. He claimed that it was during the promotion of *Homicidal* that he came across the European haunted house and decided to purchase it for a future gimmick. If this is true, then the gimmick could not have been used for *13 Ghosts* because the film was released a year prior to *Homicidal*. If Castle did purchase the house with intentions of using it as a gimmick for one of his films, it's likely it would have been for his 1963 feature *The Old Dark House*. However, the problems inherent in the gimmick would have made publicity stunt too difficult to accomplish. It will be discussed further in relation to *The Old Dark House* in Chapter 13.

The cast for *13 Ghosts* was again made up of little known actors, however it did have two noteworthy stars. Margaret Hamilton, who had risen to fame as the wicked witch in *The Wizard of Oz*, took on the role of the housekeeper, Elaine, and a young actor named Martin Milner was cast in the film as the lawyer, Ben Rush. Milner had a long list of credits to his name by the time William Castle came along and had most recently starred in Orson Welles' 1959 film *Compulsion*. But Milner would make a name for himself in television, starring in *Route 66* in 1960 and later in *Adam 12* and several other TV series and movies.

Others in the cast included Charles Herbert, Jo Morrow, Rosemary DeCamp, Donald Woods and John Van Dreelen. The real stars of the film, though, were the ghosts.

The Director Takes to the Screen Again

The film again starts off with screams and a black screen and then splashes of paint and ghoulish sounds set the stage for what's to come. But, before the opening Castle once again appears on screen to introduce his picture. Shown sitting behind a desk, Castle tells the audience about the process behind Illusion-O. At the end of the film, Castle appears once more inviting the viewers to take the glasses home with them to see if they could find more ghosts with them. It was a chance to meet his fans again and to further attach his face to the films he was creating. He would continue to do so for several more years.

The film was again a success when it was released in August 1960. In addition to the Illusion-O gimmick some theaters added their own touches using sheets in the shape of ghosts wired above audiences for added thrills.

Castle actually encouraged theater owners to be inventive in their promotion of the film. In publicity material he provided theaters with pennants to hang in lobbies and gave owners a list of stunts they could use to gain interest. The kits suggested sounds of eerie screams and cries, placing dancing ghosts in the lobby, asking local libraries to display ghost story books, and having a special "spook night" showing or scary costume contests with prizes for the best costumes. He even suggested theater owners use a stunting sky-writer to place messages in the sky or use a plane to fly around towns with a banner saying "'13 Ghosts' Coming" and the name of the theater.

In Los Angeles the director/producer set up a large clock on the side of a major highway which displayed "Pacific Ghost Time" which pointed to a 13th hour on the clock and text that read "William Castle and his supernatural associates will next haunt you with '13 Ghosts.' Now spooking at Columbia Studios." Castle even suggested theaters across the country also use the clock gimmick in the theater lobbies.

While the Illusion-O gimmick didn't generate as much commotion as Percepto, Castle had fine-tuned his persona and knew the Castle name alone would generate interest in the picture and the gimmick. By this time he had a growing fan club that would soon peak at roughly 250,000 members. Columbia had four secretaries to handle the fan mail, which was estimated at 500 letters a week, and Castle used the club as a way to generate interest in his next picture, sending out notices prior to each release.

In addition, Castle had developed a keen ability for generating publicity and reaching his fans. His main avenue was through the media. But while the traditional media panned his films and found him to be a ham, Castle took advantage of publicity from avant-garde publications like *Famous Monsters of Filmland*, a magazine for horror film fans that covered movies that many other magazines would ignore. He would also appear on local rock and roll radio stations and teen TV shows like *American Bandstand* to plug upcoming movies.

A New Direction

In the summer of 1960 Alfred Hitchcock debuted his own version of the low-budget horror film. For years directors of lesser talent, like William Castle, had been attempting to capitalize on Hitchcock's success and mirror the suspense tales he spun so well. Hitchcock turned the tables and released *Psycho*. It was a smash, earning more than $9 million at the box office—far better than anything William Castle had accomplished. And Castle's own film, *13 Ghosts,* was dwarfed by the publicity and success surrounding Hitchcock's horror.

Castle was in awe of the success of Alfred Hitchcock. He had already been mirroring his onscreen appearances and gently trying to generate some of the same suspense elements in his pictures, but now Hitchcock had given him a take on horror that was new and surprising and showed that he could beat Castle at his own game. But Castle saw it as an opportunity and soon launched into the production of his own *Psycho*.

Anyone Feeling Homicidal?

It's odd that William Castle never mentioned the influence Alfred Hitchcock's *Psycho* had on his 1961 horror *Homicidal*. Castle does credit Hitchcock with helping him develop one of the gimmicks he used for the film, but never discusses the effect *Psycho* had on him or his future filmmaking. The effect it had was indeed great and a number of Castle's later films utilized elements from the classic by the master of suspense.

Homicidal could easily be written off as a blatant copy of *Psycho* had it not mirrored the film so closely, while still developing its own tale that is, if anything, slightly more involved and developed than Hitchcock's horror. Though inferior to *Psycho*, the film did mark a change in style for William Castle and he began to evolve as a director trying various styles and genres.

While *Psycho* is a tightly-developed story with a strong elements and visual drive, *Homicidal* is an intricate story, weaker on elements and visuals, but captivating in its twists and turns. In many ways the film is more of a compliment to *Psycho* than it is a copy of it.

Reviewers have been mixed over the *Psycho/Homicidal* connection. *Time* magazine, upon the release of the Castle film, rated the film better than Hitchcock's classic—a point Castle was quick to point out in his memoirs. And other reviewers have called it the best of Castle's films with a suspenseful story that easily stands on its own without comparison to *Psycho*. Still, other reviewers call the film simply the first in a long line of *Psycho* imitators that did nothing but disparage the genre of horror by turning it merely into a wealth of films calling on gore to replace good writing and talented direction.

A Twisted Tale

Following on the heels of *13 Ghosts*, Robb White quickly crafted a story that had all the elements of a Castle picture, but obviously capitalizing on the effect *Psycho* was having across the country. Castle provided White with the necessary pieces in which the story would revolve. White himself admitted in an interview that when he finally saw *Psycho* he was embarrassed, realizing Castle's story so closely resembled Hitchcock's picture.

The story begins with an attractive blonde arriving at a hotel. She convinces the handsome bellboy to marry her for $2,000, but during the ceremony, when the justice of the peace offers to kiss the bride, after he has pronounced them husband and wife, she stabs the justice to death and runs out without her new husband. She leaves the scene and police put out a bulletin for the dangerous woman.

We soon learn the woman, whose name is Emily, lives in a large old house and takes care of a wheelchair-bound mute woman. She claims to be the wife of a man named Warren, who, on his 21st birthday, will inherit his father's estate. Warren has a half-sister who is the only other member of the family in line to inherit, but since the money is directed to go to the first-born son it appears the sister, Miriam, is out of luck.

As the story rolls forward we see Emily's hatred for both Miriam and the wheelchair-bound mute woman who happens to be Warren's nanny, the woman who helped raise him after the death of his parents. Emily's mental breakdown progresses while Miriam and her boyfriend, along with the help of Warren, try to piece together what's happening.

When the film reaches its climax we are shocked to find that Warren and Emily are the same person and an intricate scheme is uncovered. It appears that the nanny, before her illness, brought Warren/Emily into the world and because the father so desperately wanted a son, she and the child's mother conspired to keep it a secret that Warren was actually a girl. Raised as a boy, she would inherit the fortune at 21 leaving nothing for Miriam.

The only two people who knew of the cover-up were the justice of the peace, who signed the birth certificate and is killed at the beginning of the story, and the nanny who Emily has been planning to kill through much of the picture. And lastly, Emily plans to rid the world of Miriam to ensure that no one else inherits her fortune should the secret come out.

Like *Psycho*, the story features two gruesome murders. First, the justice of the peace receives numerous stabs to his abdomen and a great deal of blood makes the scene far more gory that Hitchcock's shower murder, but much less horrific.

The second murder, that of the deaf mute woman, is a decapitation. Although we never actually see the murder, we see the result when Miriam ventures into the house at the end of the picture and a shadow of the mute woman shows her head roll off her shoulders and down the stairs. It's then that Emily makes her move on Miriam and removes the wig showing both the audience and Miriam that she is both Emily and Warren. But before she can stab Miriam to death she is shot by the police and Miriam is rescued in time to inherit the fortune.

The imagry of *Psycho* appears throughout the film. In addition to the two gruesome killings, the blonde arriving at the hotel/motel mirrors the early scenes of *Psycho*. The woman, after she has committed a crime—in *Psycho*, Janet Leigh has stolen $40,000, while in *Homicidal*, Emily is wanted for murder—is pursued by the police, but escapes. The mute woman holds similar secrets to the true identity of Emily/Warren, as does the corpse of Mrs. Bates to Norman in *Psycho*. And the climax of both films features a gender-confused killer stalking a sister—Vera Miles is Janet Leigh's sister in *Psycho*, while Patricia Breslin portrays Miriam, Warren's sister, in *Homicidal*.

Left to right, Patricia Breslin, Eugenie Leontovitch, and Jean Arless
(AKA Joan Marshall) in Castle's 1961 film 'Homicidal.'

The Casting

Castle claimed the idea for the film was reportedly inspired by a real-life news story from Scandinavia in the 1950s and for the lead role of Warren/Emily, Castle was undecided whether it should be portrayed by a man or a woman.

"At first I had thought of casting an actor in the two roles," said Castle. "Interviewing many beautiful young men, most of them gay, I finally decided a man was wrong. So, scouring the theatrical offices in Hollywood, I looked for the right girl. For weeks I searched, but to no avail."

Castle claimed that an agent contacted him with the perfect girl. Castle agreed to meet her and found her "strikingly beautiful and had a strange, different quality about her."

Joan Marshall was the actress. Castle then asked Ben Lane, head of Columbia makeup, to do him a favor and try and transform Marshall into a man. "That's a tall order, Bill, even for you, but I'll do my best."

Castle said Lane's work was a success and he was convinced Marshall could handle the role. Wardrobe was used to fit her into a man's suit and her blond hair was cut and dyed to look like a man's. For the actual filming, false teeth were used to transform the structure of her face and her voice was dubbed in the scenes where she performed as Warren.

To make the transformation complete, Castle decided to change her name to Jean Arless, a somewhat androgynous name, so viewers would never be sure if the role was being portrayed by a man or a woman. Even in the final credits a split screen shows both characters were portrayed by Arless, so the public was never really sure.

Today, the secret is not as well hidden, however, in 1961 it was uncommon for a woman in drag and the secret was much better kept. Had Castle cast a man in the role it's possible the secret would not have worked as well.

In addition to Joan Marshall and Patricia Breslin, veteran actress Eugenie Leontovich was cast as the wheelchair-bound mute. Others in the cast included Glenn Corbett, Alan Bunst and Richard Rust.

For filming, the production was broken into two parts. The first section involved all the footage of Marshall as Warren. The second part included footage of her as Emily. The film was then edited in the order the story takes place.

The Gimmicks

When Castle saw *Psycho* he said that Hitchcock's requirement that filmgoers not be admitted to the feature once it began gave him an idea of his own. He decided that if Hitchcock would refuse to admit viewers he would give viewers a chance to leave. He called it "The Fright Break."

"This is the Fright Beak! You hear that sound? The sound of a heart-beat! Is it beating faster than your heart? Or slower. The heart is going to beat for another 65 seconds to allow anyone to leave this theater who is too frightened to see the end of the picture, and get your full admis-sion refunded. Ten seconds more and we go into the house. It's now or never! Five! Four! You're a brave audience! Two! One!"

The dialogue came just at the climax of the film. As Miriam is sitting in the car waiting for Warren viewers hear a clock ticking and then a heartbeat. Castle's voice comes on to give viewers one last "Fright Break" to leave the theater if they are too terrified to stay to see the end. Once the break is over Miriam ventures into the house to find the decapitation and her harrowing clash with Emily/Warren.

"Look, Bill, it's tough enough to get money at the box office these days," said one of Columbia's top brass. "Now you're suggesting we give it back."

But Castle was convinced no one would leave and miss the end of the picture. They finally agreed to a test engagement to see if the gimmick would work. The opening was held in Youngstown, Ohio. Castle said Columbia selected a place "far enough off the beaten path so no one would ever hear of my folly."

Advertisements in the local papers displayed the "Fright Break" and a large sign out in front of the theater read "MONEY-BACK GUARAN-TEE." The 3,000-seat movie house was reportedly sold out.

The first show went well, but by the second show Castle said thou-sands of people were lined up for refunds. For a moment he feared he was wrong. But then the theater manager said after the first show ended only a few people actually left the theater. Many of the kids stayed through the second show just to leave right before the end and get a full refund. The gimmick had backfired on Castle. But he decided to fix it and go on with the show.

For the nationwide release Castle did several things to promote the picture and to keep the same thing that happened in Ohio from happening again. First, theaters offered different colored tickets for the first show and second show every evening. That way, refunds could only be given to those with the correct ticket stub. And to keep the climax a secret, in advertisements for the film he was quoted as saying "Please don't reveal the ending of *Homicidal* or your friends will kill you—if they don't, I will." And finally, he decided to put a spotlight on the cowards who left.

Theaters across the country now had a "Coward's Corner." A yellow streak on the floor and a message that read "Cowards keep walking" directed frightened fans to a table with a nurse, dressed in a yellow uniform and holding a blood-pressure device, who sat there over a large sign that labeled it as the "Coward's Corner."

Any moviegoer who left the theater for a refund was subjected to the table and the test to embarrass them and they were required to sign a yellow card which read, "I am a bona fide coward." A recorded message played over and over saying, "These cowards are too frightened to see the end of *Homicidal*—Watch them shiver in the Coward's Corner. Coward…coward…coward," played on speakers nearby.

It's been reported that after this, there were few refunds because no one wanted to actually endure the treatment of the "Coward's Corner." However, again Castle was rumored to have paid his own planted moviegoers to take part in the gimmick and "chicken out" before the end of the picture.

The Reviews

While Castle claimed in his memoirs that *Homicidal* got "great reviews," when the film was released in July, 1961, just a year after *Psycho*, the fact is the reviews were mixed at best. Although, for Castle, his reviews had usually been so poor that mixed reviews probably did sound great to him.

Time magazine did offer Castle the most glowing review he had received to date. The magazine wrote that the film "was obviously made in imitation of Hitchcock's thriller," but added that "Just as obviously it surpasses its model in structure, suspense and sheer nervous drive."

Other reviewers, however, were not so kind. *The New York Times* wrote "Near the end of *Homicidal*, yesterday's horror entry at neighborhood theaters, the disembodied voice of William Castle, the producer-director, announces a 'fright break,' during which economy-minded viewers may return their tickets for a refund...If the reprieve had come before the opening of this dismal imitation of *Psycho* and Mickey Spillane, it would have been a better idea."

The *New York Herald Tribune* wrote that "Castle's shock effects are not so much of the weird or 'horror' as of the gruesome or blood-on-the-cummerbund variety."

In the end, though, the film once again pulled in audiences and enabled Castle to move forward in the genre. The picture didn't break box office records and neither it nor its gimmicks garnered as much attention as the director's earlier outings, but it has been regarded as one of the director's best features.

Ironically, the comparisons to Hitchcock's *Psycho* resulted in an amusing moment during a talk show when singer James Brown told director Hitchcock how much he enjoyed his film, *Homicidal*. The famous director supposedly threw Brown a glance that one writer said "could have withered steel."

Punishment to Fit the Crime

The filming of *Homicidal* probably presented William Castle with the most difficult use of makeup to date. The transformation of Joan Marshall into a man was remarkable, but even so, it did not pose any particular troubles during production other than the need to film her scenes as a man first and her scenes as a woman second.

For Castle's next film, makeup again played an integral part, and even though the screen time for the elaborate makeup was a fraction of the time it played in *Homicidal,* the scenes for this film were much more complex and provided Castle with a new challenge.

A Short Story Becomes a Film

In between projects, Castle took a much needed vacation in Hawaii. One afternoon while he and his wife and two daughters were enjoying the sun, poolside at the Kahala Hilton, Castle claimed he came across an interesting short story in an issue of *Playboy* magazine. It was the story of a man named Sardonicus who, while robbing his father's grave, becomes horribly disfigured when his face is frozen in a terrifying grimace, much like that of a corpse.

Castle was captivated by the story and immediately tracked down the author to obtain the film rights for the story. Not only did he obtain the film rights from author Ray Russell, but he also hired Russell to write the screenplay for the feature. (Some have reported that the story is actually and adapation of Victor Hugo's story "The Man Who Laughed.")

Castle's memoirs never address the fact that Robb White was not asked to craft the screenplay for *Mr. Sardonicus*. It was the first time since Castle ventured out on his own that White was no longer a part of his team and it presents a question as to why the change of direction.

One possible answer was White's dissatisfaction with the work he had been doing. While he was financially rewarded several times over for the success of the films he was producing with Castle, the critical praise never came and White's stories continued to receive terrible treatment from the critics. In addition to his film and television work, White was a novelist and it's possible he reached the point where he no longer wished to subject himself to the wrath of the critics.

In addition, Castle continued to receive any credit that was offered to his films. He was the familiar face and name attached to all the projects and reaped any and all benefits that came his way while White remained in the background.

White admitted that after seeing *Psycho* he was appalled at how much of Castle's story for *Homicidal* was taken from the Hitchcock classic. His disappointment with that realization may have been the final push to get him to put some distance between himself and William Castle. The two would never collaborate on a film again.

White himself admitted in one interview that he had become embarrassed by the work. "I hated them," said White. "I mean, they're so dumb! God, there's not a worm in your backbone when you get scared," he complained, referring to *The Tingler*.

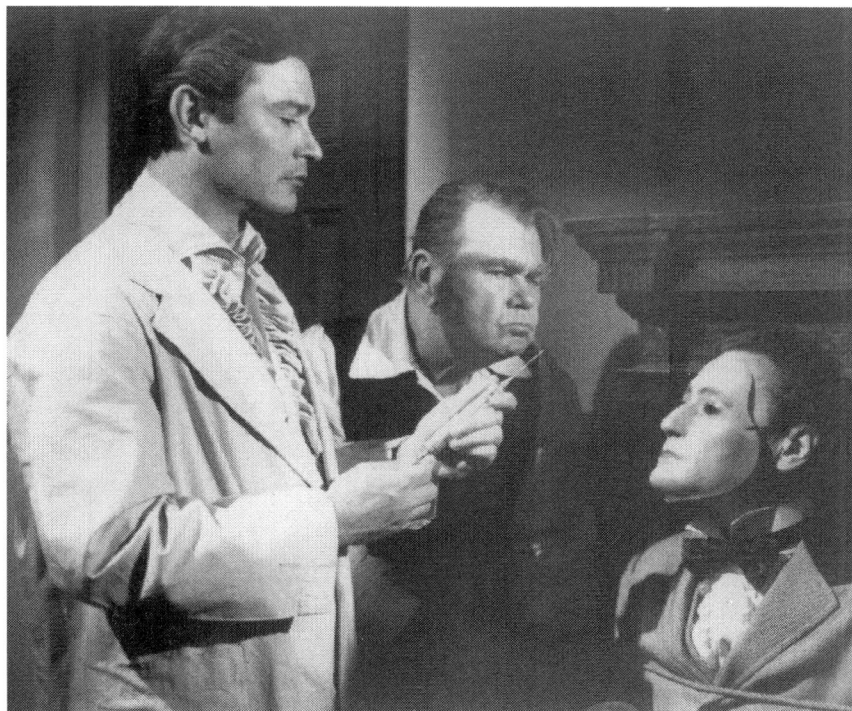

'*Mr. Sardonicus,*' in 1962, starred, left to right, Ronald Lewis, Oscar Homolka and Guy Rolfe.

The Story

Mr. Sardonicus is the story of a poor man named Marak who lives with his wife and father in a small cottage in the outskirts of England. He wants to provide his wife with luxuries he cannot afford and must live in his father's small home to make ends meet.

His father, always hoping to win the lottery, buys a lottery ticket but dies before the winning numbers are drawn. When the numbers are drawn it turns out the father held the winning ticket to wealth and riches beyond his imagination. Marak and his wife rejoice at their good fortune until they realize the ticket has been buried along with the father, tucked in his vest pocket.

The pretty young wife, Elenka, convinces her husband he must dig up the grave and return with the ticket if they are to be happy. He does so, but during the horrific deed he catches a glimpse of his father's rotting corpse and is so terrified his face becomes frozen in a distorted grimace from which he cannot recover.

Returning home the wife is appalled at her husband's face and can no longer live with him and kills herself. He claims his riches and builds a life for himself in a magnificent castle with servants and the best money can buy. He designs a leather mask to cover his terrible face and lives his life in the confines of his Castle.

He changes his name to Sardonicus after the word "sardonic," and uses his wealth to obtain a pretty young wife. She happens to love a scientist whose study of muscles leads him to a special talent for healing those who are unable to walk or use their limbs. When Sardonicus learns of this man he uses his wife to lure the man to his castle in hopes of bargaining with the young doctor. If the doctor can use his talents to heal Sardonicus' face, Sardonicus will give him his wife, who the young doctor is in love with. If he cannot, Sardonicus will torture his beautiful wife and make her as hideous as he is. The doctor agrees to help him.

The treatment is delivered, but does no good. Believing that the injury is all in his mind, the doctor tricks Sardonicus into thinking that another special treatment, using a specially created muscle relaxant from a poisonous plant, delivered to his face via a hypodermic needle, will cure him, relaxing his facial muscles back to their normal position. The treatment works and Sardonicus' face returns to normal and the doctor and wife are permitted to leave.

The doctor tells Sardonicus not to talk for a brief while to let the face heal, but a short time later Sardonicus' servant stops the doctor at the train station telling him the treatment worked, but now Sardonicus cannot move his face at all. He cannot speak, or open his mouth to eat or drink and unless something is done he will surely die.

The doctor explains to the servant that the treatment was a fake and that he only shot water into Sardonicus' face, telling him it was medicine. The injury, again, is all in his mind and the servant is urged to go back and tell him so. However, once back at the Castle, the servant lies to Sardonicus, telling him he was too late and the train had already left. It appears the servant harbors hatred for his master because of his cruel treatment of him over the years and Sardonicus is doomed to die of starvation and suffer a horrible death.

Advertisements for 'Mr. Sardonicus' promised an interactive moviegoing experience with his latest gimmick—a Punishment Poll.

The Production

Columbia Pictures once again secured a deal with Castle to market and distribute the picture and the movie was filmed on the sound stages of Hollywood which were used to recreate the look of 1880s London, the era in which the story takes place. One set included an elaborate graveyard where Sardonicus digs up his father's grave. Another sound-stage doubled for the spooky English moors and dry ice and smoke were used to create a fog that added atmosphere to the scenes.

The lead role of Sardonicus was given to an actor named Guy Rolfe. Rolfe had appeared in a numerous films. His film career began in 1947 with a role in *The Inheritance* and he appeared in more than 20 features by 1961, including *Ivanhoe* and *Snow White and the Three Stooges*.

In addition to Rolfe, Ronald Lewis took on the role of Sir Robert, the doctor asked to cure Sardonicus. Lewis also had a body of work, including 10 films, before taking part in the Castle production. The other cast members, who all had numerous credits to their name, included Audrey Dalton as Maude, Sardonicus' wife; Oskar Homolka as his servant Krull; Vladimir Sokolov was the father; and Lorna Hanson portrayed Anna, a servant in the castle.

The makeup for Rolfe required him to wear a specially-fitted mask for numerous scenes where his hideous grin is showing. The mask was attached to the lower part of his face and was a grin that was about three times Rolfe's natural smile.

Castle said that the mask was difficult to wear for Rolfe and he could only tolerate about one hour of filming at a time before he needed a break. The mask would then be removed and when production was ready to resume Rolfe would have to be refitted and makeup reapplied before filming started again. For scenes when the mask was not worn Rolfe was required to wear another mask that Sardonicus supposedly wore to hide his horrific grin. This mask enabled actor to speak, but was also hot and uncomfortable after long periods of shooting.

For actress Lorna Hanson, another scene caused discomfort when the scene called for leeches to be applied to her face. A bottle of actual leeches was brought onto the set and Castle claimed that the actress wanted nothing to do with the leeches and Hanson refused to wear them. "But their harmless," Castle claimed, putting a few on his own body to show her it was safe. When the leeches started to suck his blood and he couldn't get them off he realized she was right and sent out for artificial ones for the actual filming.

Punishment to Fit the Crime

Castle recalled in his memoirs that the production of *Mr. Sardonicus* was so much fun that it became one of his favorite pictures, but when it came time for a gimmick he wanted no part.

He claimed he wanted to step down from the throne as the King of the Gimmicks, but the studio and theater owners wouldn't let him. Giving in he devised a new plan for audience participation in the conclusion of the picture. He called it "The Punishment Poll."

Just before the final scene of *Mr. Sardonicus,* William Castle once again appears onscreen. This time he asks the audience if they believe the evil character should be punished or not. He explains that his Punishment Poll will allow them to participate in the conclusion of the film by deciding the fate of *Mr. Sardonicus.* When moviegoers entered the theater before the show they were each given a card and activated the card at an "Activator Booth" in the lobby. The card had a hand on it in the form of a closed fist with the thumb protruding. When held upright the thumb faces the ceiling and the word "Mercy" was shown. When held in the other direction the thumb faced the floor and "No Mercy" was shown.

Castle would then ask those in the theater to hold up their cards so the votes could be counted. He began counting onscreen pretending to actually be counting cards in the theater.

"Mr. Sardonicus" Punishment Poll

↑ *This side UP for NO MERCY!* ↑

↓ *This side UP for MERCY!* ↓

Punishment Poll
"Mr. Sardonicus"

The Punishment Poll for 'Mr. Sardonicus' promised a chance to vote for the outcome of the movie. In reality, there was only one ending to the film.

One Ending or Two?

Now, Castle for many years continued to claim that there were actually two endings to the film—one that showed Sardonicus mercy and one that did not. His memoirs state that Columbia did not like his original ending where the main character suffers at the end and asked him to shoot another. He decided that would be his gimmick and the audience would decide. He also claimed that ushers in the theater actually counted the raised cards and the proper ending would be shown. Castle said it did not amaze him that the crowds were almost always "bloodthirsty" and his ending won out. To this day, no alternate ending has been uncovered and it appears that there was actually only one ending to the film, the one in which the star suffers.

Director Joe Dante recalled in an interview that *Mr. Sardonicus* was his favorite Castle film and was the first truly interactive motion picture. "Of course, there was only one ending," said Dante. "and only one piece of film with Castle counting. They always ran the same footage at the end."

Loudspeakers outside the theater promoted the interactive stunt. Moviegoers in line for tickets heard a voice say, "Have you ever envied the thrill-hungry Roman crowds in the Circus Maximus who, with the wave of a thumb, could make life or death decisions that sealed the fate of many a gladiator? The fate of that ghoulish character Sardonicus is in your tender little hands. You have the opportunity of literally deciding the monstrous fiend's fate."

Teen-age fans again turned out to make the film a success, but the genre was beginning to show signs of decline and Castle was beginning to think about trying his hand at another kind of picture. But would the audience accept it? Time would tell.

A Change of Pace

In 1962, William Castle released only one picture and followed it with two features in 1963. Following up his string of horrors, Castle decided to try his had at comedy, hoping the public would accept his desire to expand into other genres. They didn't.

Zotz!

Castle had a copy of a 1946 novel by Walter Karig in his attic and claimed he always thought the story would make a good movie, so he went about rummaging through an old trunk until he found it and sat down to reread the book. Still believing it would make a good movie, and looking for the right project to transition from horror, Castle acquired the film rights and decided the comedy fit the bill. He called the story "refreshingly delightful."

Having enjoyed his work on *Mr. Sardonicus*, Castle again turned to writer Ray Russell and asked him to craft the script. Russell accepted. Castle began to move ahead with the project, but said shortly after acquiring the film rights he received a call from Walt Disney who was hoping to buy the rights from him in order to make a Disney film from the story. Castle says he declined the offer, but often wondered if he had made the right decision.

Castle was concerned how about the change of pace. In his memoirs he wrote that his biggest concern was that his fans would not accept his departure from horror into comedy, and that it was only after "deliberating for many days" that he decided to take the risk.

It appears that this was not the first comedy project he considered. According to one source, in the summer of 1960 Castle was considering doing a film entitled *Rip Van Winkle in the 21st Century*. The project never came together, but the desire to try comedy stayed in Castle's mind.

'Zotz,' starring Tom Poston, was Castle's foray into comedy in the early 60s. Released in 1962, the film was panned by most critics. Poston again went to work for Castle in his 1963 remake of 'The Old Dark House.'

Going for Laughs

Zotz! is the story of a college archeology professor, played by Tom Poston, who finds a magic coin that gives him power over everything and everyone in his path. By holding the coin in one hand and pointing with his other, the professor simply says the word "zotz" and he can do anything he wishes. He tries to share the power with the U.S. military, but they ignore him thinking he's crazy. His discovery then becomes of interest to foreign agents, who want to steal the power and capture the professor. He escapes and a chase ensues.

Humor comes from the professors ability to stop people in their tracks, slow down military tanks, stop guns from shooting and more. When the movie reaches its climax the coin is lost and the government, now realizing it misjudged the professor, mounts a massive search for the coin.

Tom Poston was given the starring role in his first feature film for *Zotz!* Poston, who went on to a long and successful television career with roles on *Newhart, Grace Under Fire* and numerous other television shows, was a young comedian in the early stages of a bright career. Even at that time his main claim to fame came in the new medium of television. Early appearances on *The U.S. Steel Hour* in 1953 and *The Phil Silvers Show* in 1955 were followed by fame as a panelist on the game show *To Tell The Truth* in 1956. He also found celebrity status from his place on *The Steve Allen Show* starting in 1956. *Zotz!* presented him with a chance to cross over to the big screen as a leading man.

In addition to Poston, Castle recruited Jim Backus, one of the stars of *Macabre* to work with him again. Others in the cast included well-known character actor Cecil Kellaway and actors Margaret Dumont, Fred Clark and Julia Meade.

In Need of a Gimmick

Prior to the release of *Zotz!*, Castle decided another gimmick was needed. Giving up the horror genre was one thing, but giving up the gimmick was another. Although he admitted he was tiring of his title as King of the Gimmicks, Castle knew that the uncharted waters of comedy for him was risky and to ensure an audience would turn out he needed a gimmick.

To promote the film the studio took out billboards in key cities that simply said "Zotz!" In addition, Castle explained in his memoirs that both bumper stickers and buttons saying "Zotz" were also distributed throughout major cities weeks before the film was to premiere weeks to generate interest in the picture.

Then, as a final push for promotion Castle had millions of gold plastic *Zotz!* coins produced and used his fan clubs to distribute most of them. By the time the film was released Castle claimed that thousands of teen-agers were waiting to see the film and find out the story behind the coin. "My worries about doing comedy completely disappeared," said Castle.

Jim Backus, one of the stars of 'Zotz!' had already starred opposite James Dean in 'Rebel Without a Cause,' and would go onto further fame as a castaway in 'Gilligan's Island.'

The Reviews Are in

Even so, it's hard to call the film a success. While box office returns on the film are hard to come by, it's apparent the film did not break any records or garner much attention when it was released in October, 1962. And while Castle was used to receiving terrible treatment at the hands of the critics, the reviews must have caused him some discomfort. His foray into comedy was received with equal disdain as his horror films.

The New York Times wrote, "Television's rubber-faced Tom Poston has lost his bounce in the shift from living room to movie house. For that matter, his partners in yesterday's new neighborhood theater entry called *Zotz!*, Julia Meade and Jim Backus, also looked a lot happier on the home screen…The flaccid farce chosen as a showcase for their video-trained talents is the handiwork of William Castle, a producer more familiar with low-budget horror fare."

And if that was not bad enough, reviewer Eugene Archer closed the review by saying, "The coin's most potent power, however, was its ability to afflict every onlooker with an acute case of indigestion. The film needs no such magic powers to produce the same effect."

Another Teaming with Poston

Even with some tough reviews, the film didn't get all bad reviews. It's also been called a "charming, underrated little fantasy" and the film enabled Castle moved ahead with another project which again starred Tom Poston. This time, however, Castle stepped into more familiar territory with a story that combined both comedy and horror. It was a remake of a 1932 classic called *The Old Dark House*.

This time he could provide his fans with something closer to what they were expecting while still exploring his interest in comedy. Castle also had a gimmick ready for the picture, but apparently passed on the opportunity.

As mentioned earlier in this book, Bill Castle claimed he purchased an old castle in Europe in the early 1960s with the intention of giving the house away as a gimmick for one of his pictures. In his memoirs he claimed that the house was acquired during a promotion tour for *Homicidal*. During the trip Castle visited England, Germany, France,

Holland, Belgium and Spain. While in France he saw the house and the gimmick was born.

Castle claimed the gimmick was planned for *13 Ghosts*, however, *13 Ghosts* was released in August 1960 and the promotional tour for *Homicidal* could not have taken place until after that film's release in July 1961, so the gimmick must have been acquired for use in another picture. *The Old Dark House* would have been the ideal vehicle, but Castle's memoirs never discuss the film or any gimmick he might have had for it.

If the house idea was considered for the film's release the idea was dropped before the picture hit theaters because *The Old Dark House* did not use an actual gimmick to attract its audience.

Castle's intention was to have 20 million keys made for the lock to the front door of his supposed haunted castle. Only one key would actually fit and each filmgoer would have had the chance of getting the key to the castle. The idea was fraught with difficulty because it would be impossible for every moviegoer to make a trip to Europe to see if their key was the key that opened the door. And it would have been nearly impossible to keep track of all the keys or the one key that actually unlocked the door. Because of the difficulties it's easy to see why the gimmick never made it to the movie house.

The only unique selling point for the picture was that Castle released the film the day before Halloween, just in time to draw the holiday fans out for some thrills and laughs. In addition to Poston, the film starred Robert Morley, Janette Scott, Joyce Grenfell, Peter Bull and Fanella Fielding.

A Reworking of a Classic

The story, based on the novel *Benighted* by J.B. Priestly, was adapted for the screen by Robert Dillon and centers around Poston's character Tom Penderel. Penderel, a used car salesman, is an

American who, during a storm, is forced to seek shelter in the old home of a wealthy family in Europe. Called Femm Hall, the forbidding place is home to numerous members of the Femm family. When Poston arrives he is warned to leave before he gets himself murdered. The warning comes for Cecily Femm, who appears to be the most normal of the family members.

Apparently, the members of the Femm family are being murdered off one by one by an unknown killer hoping to get the family inheritance. We eventually come to learn that Cecily, the apparently normal one, is actually the murderer. But before she can do away with Poston and everyone else left in the house she is killed herself by one of her instruments of death—an exploding clock.

Filmed in England, the feature was actually a production of Hammer Films, a low-budget production company known mostly for its gothic horror pictures. Columbia released the picture in the United States.

"My idea was to combine two entertainment factors—thrills and laughs—into a single package," Castle told one interviewer. "Looking at it from another point of view, the comedy-thriller is also easier to sell. You can sell it three different ways—as a comedy, as a thriller, or as both."

Castle's problem was probably that he tried to sell it at all.

The Release

Released on October 30, 1963, *The Old Dark House* was both a critical and a box office failure. *The New York Times* barely found room to review the feature at all. Part of a double-bill, Columbia released the picture along with another horror picture called *Maniac*.

While *Maniac* actually received mediocre reviews, *The Old Dark House* was not so lucky. *The Times* called it "a laboriously arch and broad blend of humor and the creeps. It still leaves the old J.B. Priestly property as dead as a doornail. Even a picturesque cast, headed by Tom

Poston, Robert Morley, Janette Scott and especially, Joyce Grenfell, can't rejuvenate it."

An interesting footnote to the story is that *The Old Dark House* was filmed in color, but the release was in black and white. Still, when it occasionally finds its way onto television, the color print is often used.

As for Castle, he wasn't finished yet. He still had something to prove and had another idea already in progress.

13 Frightened Girls

Sandwiched between *Zotz!* and *The Old Dark House* was another film that provided Castle with somewhat of a departure from his usual displays of horror. The 1963 film, *13 Frightened Girls*, offered Castle elements of comedy, horror and adventure, all wrapped up in a title he could sell to the public.

While not necessarily appropriate to the film, the title gave the impression the feature was more horrific than it actually was. The deception itself was a gimmick for Castle who had all along been promising features that could scare viewers to death or frighten them so much they'd need to leave the theater. In reality the films were usually less frightening than promised.

For this outing, *13 Frightened Girls* promised to deliver a few jolts and even a few corpses, along with humor and suspense, but most of all the film resembled the international espionage adventure genre that James Bond had brought to the movie scene.

The film is based on a story by *New York Herald Tribune* film critic Otis L. Guernsy, Jr. Entitled *The Candy Web* in its worldwide release, the film was released in the U.S. as *13 Frightened Girls* to capitalize on Castle's horror notoriety. The film centers around the lives of a group of girls at an exclusive boarding school in Switzerland. The girls are all daughters of international diplomats working in London who send the girls to the same boarding school. The girls are each privy to top secrets from their respective countries and become involved in international intrigue when one of the girls, the U.S. diplomat's daughter, begins masquerading as a secret agent named "Kitten."

Kitten uncovers a plot by communist Chinese government officials who are using a mole to infiltrate the U.S. embassy in London to frame a top agent for murder. Kitten uncovers a dead body in the basement meat locker of a Chinese diplomat's residence and the victim was apparently murdered with a letter opener from the U.S. embassy. Kitten escapes via a dumb waiter and takes the incriminating evidence with her saving her embassy from involvement in an international incident. She anonymously returns the opener to the embassy with a letter signed "Kitten." She then begins helping on other diplomatic troubles and the secret agents begin to wonder who this "Kitten" is. The communists want to eliminate her and she is then nearly killed when another agent drugs her and tries to throw her off a building. She again manages to escape.

As the movie reaches its climax a pair of agents who have been hired to kill her are outwitted when all the girls join forces in their same school uniform and the agents can't uncover the one they want before she escapes. After a few more twists and turns, the girl is rescued by a U.S. agent and the International incident is covered up.

13 Gimmicks in One

Bill Castle was well aware of the international film market. With most of his releases he participated in international tours and premieres to promote his films and was even thrilled when he had the opportunity to hear himself dubbed into other languages for filmed introductions that accompanied several of his pictures. For *13 Frightened Girls* he found a way to take advantage of the international market by using girls from different countries to star in the picture.

"[I]t'll be an international smash," He explained to a studio executive. "Each girl will be the star of the picture in her own country. Her name will go on the marquee. For example, in Germany we'll star the German girl, France the French girl, in Japan the Japanese girl, and so on. Think of the publicity we'll get around the world. I'll contact the leading magazine or newspaper in each country, talk them into running a talent search for the perfect teen-ager to represent them."

When the executive began to get concerned about cost issues. Castle explained that the publicity would be free. And he managed to get the airlines to foot the bill for the girls' airfare. The contest ran for eight weeks with thousands of entries. The production offered all expenses paid for the girl and a chaperone, $300 in spending money and a complete wardrobe from a leading fashion house in each girl's country.

The selected girls arrived in Hollywood and each was greeted personally by Castle and then driven to the Montecito Hotel in Hollywood, their home during production. The girls had a weekend of touring the city and production began on Monday morning.

Castle recalled in his memoirs that the production was troubled from the start because interpreters were needed to translate the communications for several girls and a few had demands for equal screen time with the others in the film. Castle said it was like a United Nations session and for each girl who didn't know English, they were basically fed lines which the repeated directly back to the camera. It wasn't actually acting, but they managed.

Much of the film was shot in Arrowhead, California, Castle claimed, with a nearby hotel doubling for some of the interior sets, including the boarding school in Switzerland. Castle claimed that the occasional temper flared and there was a hair-pulling match between two of the girls, but overall they worked hard and the filming took place without any major international incidents.

For the release, Castle attended the premiere with each girl in her respective country. Promotions listed her as the star and Castle made it appear so with one simple twist on film. When the film opens the story is being narrated by one of the girls who is driving the bus to the airport as the girls start a vacation. Castle filmed the scene 13 different times, one with each girl driving the bus and narrating the story in her own language. Each girl then had the chance to star in her own film.

While the film could hardly be listed as one of Castle's greatest successes, like the other two features, *13 Frightened Girls* enabled Castle to explore new avenues in movie making. It is also notable as the first film released in color of his series as a producer. But the poor reviews and returns at the box office of his recent films led Castle to return to the genre he knew best. And this time he had a star leading the way.

Anyone Got an Ax?

By 1962 Joan Crawford was a legend. She was one of the few stars who emerged from silent films with a career in talkies that flourished. During her years at MGM she was continually one of the leading, if not the leading, box office stars at the studio.

When the studio let her go in the mid-1940s it was sure she was washed up. Crawford showed them all when she turned around and won an Oscar for leading actress in Warner Bros. *Mildred Pierce* in 1945. She followed the film with several more Academy Award-nominated performances and numerous box office hits like *Humoresque, Possessed* and *Sudden Fear*.

By the late 50s she was well passed her prime, and although the roles were getting harder to come by, she managed to find work in films like *The Story of Esther Costello* and *The Best of Everything*.

When the 1960s dawned things were somewhat difficult. She was recently widowed when her husband, Alfred Steele, an executive with Pepsi-Cola Company, died suddenly. And although he was a successful business man, in reality he left her in debt having borrowed $100,000 from her shortly before his death. She needed to work.

She filled her husband's spot on the Pepsi board, but still needed work in Hollywood. And in 1962 she found a project that she thought was ideal. It was the story of two aging actresses living in an old house in Hollywood, one crippled and the other a bit off her rocker. It was a dark film, a bit horrific, and a challenge for any actress. Crawford wanted it as a project for both her and Bette Davis, an actress she had admired and longed to work with. She convinced director Robert Aldrich, whom she had worked with on *Autumn Leaves*, to direct the project and Davis agreed the vehicle was a good one.

All the studios rejected the project, thinking it would bomb at the box office because Davis and Crawford no longer had selling power. A young production house, Seven Arts, agreed to take a chance and the film was distributed by Warner Bros. The film was *What Ever Happened to Baby Jane?* and it was a smash.

The actresses accepted salaries below their normal wage in exchange for a cut of the profits. The deal payed off for both women when the film pulled in millions. It also launched them back into the spotlight and reignited their careers.

The problem was that even though the actresses were now sought after commodities, the material focused on the horror genre. And it not only opened up the genre for Davis and Crawford, but numerous other aging actresses were finding themselves working again in horror pictures.

Both Crawford and Davis signed onto a sequel called *Hush Hush Sweet Charlotte*, but Crawford bowed out early due to reported illness, although rumors hinted that the difficulty of working with Davis was her real reason for leaving. She was replaced by Olivia De Havilland and the film was finished without her.

The film went on to be a success, but not at the level of *Baby Jane*. But by then Crawford had moved on as well—onto the lead in William Castle's next production, a shocker called *Strait-Jacket*.

In Need of a Star

Castle returned to horror in 1963 with a production that he hoped would put him on the same playing field as Alfred Hitchcock. Robert Bloch, author of the novel on which Hitchcock based *Psycho*, was hired to craft the screenplay for *Strait-Jacket*. It had many of the same elements of Hitchcock's hit and Bloch tried to add in enough blood, gore and macabre humor to make the film sell to horror fans. But what Castle needed was a star.

The first actress signed to the role, suprisingly enough, was not Joan Crawford. Joan Blondell, best known for her comedic supporting roles opposite major stars like Katherine Hepburn and Spencer Tracy in *Desk Set*, or starring opposite John Wayne in *Lady for a Night*, had not starred in a major picture in some time. Castle would have had no difficulty in signing her to the role, but might have feared she would not be able to sell the picture. Castle, however, was used to working with gimmicks, not stars, to sell his pictures, so he moved ahead with Blondell in the lead.

Blondell was actually preparing actively for the role and had even been fitted for costumes, but before production could begin an accident at home altered her plans. "I stepped through a glass partition in my home and had to have 60 stitches in my leg," reported Blondell.

With Blondell's injury pulling her out of the picture Castle needed a replacement fast. One evening Castle found himself face to face with Joan Crawford during a party in Beverly Hills. Another person as the party that evening said Castle practically "fell at her feet." He introduced himself and launched into his offer. He told her he had a script written by *Psycho* author Robert Bloch and even claimed it was written specifically with her in mind.

Crawford told Castle to go on and as he explained the story she expressed interest in the project. "She is a suspected killer and she believes it herself," explained Castle to Crawford.

"And?" said Crawford.

"She is arrested. But she's not the killer. It's her twisted daughter," replied Castle.

"The little bitch." responded Crawford, who then asked when she could see a script.

Castle sent Crawford the script and set up a meeting with her to discuss the project. Castle and writer Bloch were invited to Crawford's New York apartment for lunch to discuss the details. Arriving at noon, they were welcomed by Crawford herself at the door and ushered in to her apartment. She asked them to remove their shoes, as she did all her guests, not wanting to dirty her carpets. Over lunch she told them she liked the script, but "*Strait-Jacket* will have to be entirely rewritten as a vehicle for me, or I will not accept the role."

Castle claimed the script had to be totally rewritten from scratch, but it was worth it to get Joan Crawford as his star. One of the changes included changing the age of her character. In the original, she was to age from 30 to 50, but Crawford required her character to be younger, asking that five years be dropped off. They agreed. In addition, Crawford demanded approval over not only the script, but the cast and crew and the cameraman. When they agreed to all her demands she signed on at a salary of $50,000 and a percentage of the profits. And Hollywood was furious.

Actually, it wasn't so much as Hollywood as it was Bette Davis. Davis and Crawford were both competitive and had a long rivalry in Hollywood. When Davis found out Joan Crawford had replaced Joan Blondell she accused her of back-stabbing.

"…Crawford stepped in and stole the role," Davis exclaimed to gossip columnist Louella Parsons.

Parsons confirmed that Blondell was assigned the role and even fitted for costumes, then accused Crawford of stealing Blondell's part. "Then out of the blue, producer William Castle signs the other Joan. And then he proceeds to turn his picture upside down to please her. Even the crew has been revamped, with a new cameraman, makeup man, hairdresser, costumer—even a switch in publicity man. No one involved is talking," said Parsons.

Bette Davis added, "There is an unwritten law in this town. Once an actor is signed for a part, it's theirs until they die or drop out voluntarily. Miss Crawford knows this and should be ashamed of herself."

The issue blew over, but it wasn't until many years later that Blondell actually admitted she left the part voluntarily due to injury. In 1977, the year both Crawford and Castle died, Blondell explained, "Nothing was said in the papers, because of the insurance, but Joan Crawford did not steal the role. Someone had to do it."

The Production

During the weeks of pre-production Castle wondered if he had bit off more than he could chew. Would Joan Crawford be more than he could handle, he wondered? He recalled that her demands were excessive and she was somewhat of a perfectionist. But because he admired her and usually agreed that her ideas on the film were right, he bowed to her requests and production moved along.

Crawford requested that associate producer Dona Holloway fly to New York so the star's wardrobe could be purchased there. Castle agreed and Holloway found that Joan was "a pussycat." Crawford and Holloway developed a friendship during production that would last until Crawford's death nearly 15 years later.

"Joan asked me when you plan to start rehearsals," asked Holloway to Castle.

"Rehearsals?" hollered Castle. "Who said anything about rehearsals? I just want to start shooting…No goddamn rehearsals. I never have rehearsals before I shoot."

But this time he would. On an empty stage with only folding chairs, the cast began rehearsals for the film. An unknown actress was initially cast in the role of Crawford's daughter, but when she appeared too nervous and unable to deliver her lines opposite the legendary star, Joan demanded that she be replaced.

"Speak up dear," Crawford pleaded with the young actress. But when she failed to perform Crawford took Castle aside and told him they had to "get rid of her" for the sake of the picture. Castle admitted the star was right and fired the actress.

Crawford herself might have had something to do with her replacement. Diane Baker, a young actress who had first worked with Crawford in 1959's *The Best of Everything* was hired for the part. Her ability to work with Crawford on an eye-to-eye level provided mutual respect for the actors and Castle claimed "Crawford sensed this, and together they made the words in the script come to life."

The additional cast included Leif Erickson as Crawford's brother, Rochelle Hudson as his wife, George Kennedy as the handyman and Mitchell Cox, a real-life vice president for Pepsi-Cola, who portrayed Joan's doctor.

Shortly before production, Castle claimed Rock Hudson had called and asked him if he could find a small part for a young actor he thought showed promise. Castle had worked with Hudson years before and agreed to find a place for the new actor. Cast in the role of Joan's two-timing husband, Lee Majors, who later went onto fame as *The Six-Million Dollar Man*, got his start in the first few moments of the picture, before he gets his head chopped off.

The story follows the troubles of Lucy Harbin, who returns home one evening and kills her husband and his mistress when she catches them in bed together. Using an ax, she chops their heads off before the eyes of her young daughter and is then carried off to the madhouse wearing a strait-jacket, of course. Her daughter is sent to live with Lucy's brother and his wife. Flash-forward 20 years and Lucy Harbin is released from the mental hospital, cured, and returns home to live with her brother and to try and rekindle the relationship with her daughter.

Not used to life in the real world, Lucy begins to unravel and shows signs of a breakdown. Family pictures in a photo album are cut up, removing all the heads of her husband, and Lucy starts hearing voices and finds severed heads in her bed at night. But when others investigate, the heads are gone and no one is around the hear the voices chant "Lucy Harbin took and ax…gave her husband 40 whacks. When she saw what she had done…she gave his girlfriend 41."

Lucy's doctor pays her a visit and rethinks her release, but before he can carry her back to the hospital he is murdered. Several other brutal ax murders occur as well leading viewers to suspect that Lucy has returned to her old ways. In the end it is revealed that Lucy's daughter has actually gone insane and was committing the murders trying to frame her mother and get her put away for good. As the movie closes, the daughter is carted off to an asylum and Lucy promises to stick by her and help her through her recovery.

Filming went well, but for the early scenes in which Lucy's daughter Carol witnesses her father's murder, a young girl, looking like Diane Baker, was needed for filming. Castle claimed that Crawford suggested Castle use his own daughter, Terry, because she held a strong resemblance to Baker. Castle asked his wife and daughter and brought her in for the filming, but she was frightened and unable to do the scene, even when they gave Crawford a baseball bat to hold instead of an ax. In the end another little girl was hired for the brief part.

Castle also claimed one of the other difficulties with production was coming up with the proper sound a head would make when it was chopped off. He claimed they considered a block of wood and a wet telephone book before they settled on chopping a watermelon. He even joked that he tried to find a tie-in with the Gillette Razor Company for a gimmick for the film, but the president hung up on him when he suggested a slogan like "Go see *Strait-Jacket* and then cut your head off with a Gillette."

Diane Baker and Joan Crawford starred in Castle's 1964 hit 'Strait-Jacket.'

The Star Becomes the Gimmick

Castle finally felt he had a horror film that was not in need of a gimmick to promote itself, although he did succumb to several publicity stunts to draw fans to the theater. First and foremost, the star herself was the gimmick used to sell *Strait-Jacket*. Crawford, who had a stake in the profits, agreed to a tour of the major cities where the movie premiered, to promote the film.

Crawford's position on the Pepsi board and the company's executive Mitchell Cox's role in the film enabled the star to use Pepsi's corporate jet to fly across the country for the tour. In each city where she appeared, a large bus containing 28 pieces of luggage and food hampers was used to transport the star. Her maid, a photographer, a publicity man and two pilots were along for the ride. At each theater well-known columnist Dorothy Kilgallen introduced Crawford, who would then take the stage holding the same large ax used in the picture. She would do a brief question and answer period with the columnist and take a few questions from the crowd. The picture would then begin and Crawford and her entourage would head off for the next premiere. Radio, TV and newspaper spots promoted both the film and Crawford's live appearances. The gimmick worked and the film was a success.

In addition to the star, the promotion of the picture focused on the horrific elements by using two slogans. The first, "Warning: *Strait-Jacket* vividly depicts ax murders" highlighted the decapitations, which would surely draw young fans to the picture. Older fans of Crawford hopefully would turn out for her performance. The second slogan, "Keep telling yourself it's only a movie" promised horror unlike anything moviegoers had been shown before and the slogan was so catchy that several films have used the same phrase since. To seal the deal, Castle gave in to the gimmicks and produced millions of small cardboard axes with fake blood on them to hand out to ticket buyers.

The film was released in January 1964 and Castle called the box office success "dazzling," but admitted that the film still had not elevated him above the standard horror exploitation film. Reviews, he said were mostly favorable, but even so, they were hardly glowing.

While *Variety* said "Miss Crawford does well by her role, delivering an animated performance," *The Daily News* said she was "hampered by a script riddled with clichés."

Elaine Rothschild of *Films in Review* said, "I must say I am full of admiration for Joan Crawford, for even in drek like this she gives a performance."

And finally, the *New York Herald Tribune* wrote, "Strait-Jacket should be subtitled *What Ever Happened to Baby Monster?* and there's a clue for you. [It] proves that lightning does not strike twice and that it's time to get Joan Crawford out of those housedress horror B movies and back in haute couture. Miss Crawford, you see, is high class, Too high class to withstand in mufti the banality of Robert Bloch's script, cheap-jack production, inept and/or vacuous supporting players and direction better suited to the mist-and-cobweb idiocies of the Karloff school of suspense."

One of Crawford's most pleasing results of the film was that following *Baby Jane*, Bette Davis also made a shocker released about the same time as *Strait-Jacket*, and of the two features, the Joan Crawford shocker fared better at the box office. Most claimed it was due to Crawford's promotion and not that the film was any better than Davis' *Dead Ringer*. Bette Davis remarked, "She criticized me for raffling off dolls onstage for *Baby Jane* and she's got a goddamn ax under her skirt?"

A Living Nightmare

With 1964 turning into a banner year, following the success of *Strait-Jacket*, Castle needed a follow-up to keep the momentum. It had been several years since he'd had a success and he must have been happy to find there was life in the genre that had given him fame and fortune. And with his spirits high, Castle once again exited Columbia, this time for a deal to produce several features for Universal Pictures.

MCA completed its takeover of Universal in 1962, moving away from Hollywood talent agency to production house. The studio, which had primarily been successful in television, continued its efforts in the movie business with hits like *Spartacus* in 1960, *Charade* with Audrey Hepburn and Cary Grant in 1962, and Alfred Hitchcock's *The Birds* in 1963.

Hitchcock himself might have been the lure Castle saw when the master of suspense moved over to Universal Pictures in 1962. Although not nearly on the same playing field as Hitchcock, who at that time was actually MCA's third largest stockholder and had his pick of projects at the studio, the move did enable Castle to set up his own small production house on the studio lot. His small company within Universal included 20 employees who were under contract to him for his films alone.

He also developed a merchandising company that designed his logo, which again pays tribute to Hitchcock and his famous profile logo. The logo was a silhouette of Castle in a director's chair with his famous cigar trademark protruding from his mouth. The merchandising business licensed his name and image for use on T-shirts, games, toys, Halloween masks and a line of horror greeting cards, in addition to the promotion of his motion pictures.

The Night Walker was the project Castle chose to follow *Strait-Jacket*. Once again, Robert Bloch was hired to craft the screenplay of a story about the fine line between dreams and reality. Castle didn't want it to be a strict horror film, but follow more along Hitchcock's line of suspense. He also wanted to once again cross over his from his traditional films that attracted strictly teens to a film that pulled in an older crowd as well. Like *Strait-Jacket*, he wanted a star, or perhaps two stars, from Hollywood's heyday.

Barbara Stanwyck and Robert Taylor, once real-life husband and wife came together once again, onscreen this time, for Castle's, 'The Night Walker.' It was Stanwyck's last big screen appearance.

The Leading Lady

One of William Castle's earliest memories of his first days in Hollywood was walking onto the set of a film called *Golden Boy*. The Columbia feature was in production when Castle first started at the studio and a young Bill Castle recalled meeting William Holden who was also starting out in the film business.

Holden was one of the stars of *Golden Boy* and when Castle arrived on the set he saw the young man. "He seemed ill at ease, and frightened," Castle recalled. "Whispering, I tried to reassure him in Harry Cohn fashion. 'Relax kid. It's my first day too. I'm Bill Castle. I have a seven-way contract. What do you do?' "

"I'm William Holden and I'm supposed to be an actor, but at the present moment I have grave doubts."

Castle wrote in his memoirs that Holden then began rehearsing with Barbara Stanwyck and he was impressed with her style. "It was his first picture and it was heartwarming to see Stanwyck give him confidence. Her patience and understanding completely relaxed Holden, and as a result he gave a strong performance. Barbara Stanwyck is not only a superstar, but a great lady."

Now, 25 years later, in 1964, Castle approached Stanwyck for the starring role in his next picture. Stanwyck had finished work on her last film, *Roustabout*, costarring Elvis Presley when Castle approached her about the project. "I heard from Mr. Castle—'round about March or April—and he said, 'I have a good screenplay. At least I think it's good. Will you read it?' I said I would be delighted to read it," Stanwyck recalled saying.

Stanwyck was not known for works like *The Night Walker*, but shortly before the role came up she had passed on another opportunity and might have regretted it. When Joan Crawford stepped out of *Hush...Hush, Sweet Charlotte* director Robert Aldrich sent the script to several leading ladies to take her place—Barbara Stanwyck was included on the short list. She considered it but was hesitant at taking part in the Bette Davis shocker. Olivia De Havilland took the role and the film was a success. This time she didn't hesitate.

Stanwyck said she was fascinated by the story and agreed to do it. Castle had some concern about Stanwyck's costar, but decided to approach her and ask her what she thought. "I had a wonderful idea and I want to throw it at you and see what you think," said Castle to Stanwyck during a phone conversation. "What do you think of Robert Taylor in the part of the attorney?"

"Well, I think it's wonderful but you'd better ask Mr. Taylor how he feels about it," replied Stanwyck.

Barbara Stanwyck and Robert Taylor had been two of Hollywood's brightest stars. When they married in May 1939 it was a famous Hollywood union and their fans were caught up in it. They divorced in early 1951, but in time managed to rekindle their friendship. However, by the mid-60s Taylor was married again and Stanwyck reportedly told Castle that in addition to getting Robert Taylor's permission he might want to make sure it was ok with his current wife.

Robert Taylor reportedly was hesitant about doing the picture, but his wife Ursula convinced him it was a good idea and he accepted the part. Ursual Taylor, interestingly enough, had a history with Castle, having worked for him years before when he directed her in *The Iron Glove* in 1954.

When Taylor greeted the press to tell them about teaming with his former wife again, he said, "Any actor who would turn down a chance to play opposite Barbara Stanwyck, under any circumstances, would have to be out of his head. She's certainly one of the pros in the business. I'm very enthusiastic about the film. It looks like it will be a pleasant experience."

Castle was also thrilled about the team and knew that bringing Barbara Stanywck and Robert Taylor together again was cause for promotion. In announcing the pairing, Castle told the press, "I consider this one of the most dramatic castings of many years. I couldn't be more pleased that these two great stars consented to do this drama for me."

Joan Crawford's financial return on *Strait-Jacket* proved to be a good move for the star and the director. He was able to pay her a minimal salary in promise of a return for the success of the release. This drove Crawford to do everything in her power to make the film a success and when it was both she and Castle reaped the rewards. For *The Night Walker,* a similar deal was negotiated.

For the picture, both Stanwyck and Taylor agreed to work for scale in return for a percentage of the box office receipts. Stanwyck also agreed to mount a promotional tour for the film upon its release, similar to Crawford's.

The Sleepless Tale

Production on the film took place in late summer, 1964. The story centers around Stanwyck's character, Irene Trent, a woman whose blind, possessive and jealous husband makes her life such hell that her dreams of a tall, handsome stranger seem real. The husband suspects her of having an affair with his lawyer, Barry Morland, played by Robert Taylor, and hires a private detective to find out.

When the husband is killed in an explosion Irene is allowed to return to the house, but the room where the explosion occurred is locked off because a gaping hole in the floor poses a threat to her safety.

Irene begins having nightmares, hearing the explosion and seeing her husband's charred face, and decides she can no longer live in the house. She wants to sell it, but Barry tells her the estate will be tied up for some time. To get away she moves into a small apartment behind a beauty parlor she owns. Still, the dreams continue to haunt her and a handsome man, played by Lloyd Bochner, shows up and takes her to an apartment and then a chapel where they are married before a priest and witnesses made of wax.

Not sure if her dreams are real or in her imagination she asks Barry to help her find out. They discover the apartment and the chapel, but nothing looks the same and she's still not sure.

Sure enough, the dream is real and Bochner is the detective hired by the husband to follow Irene. He happens to be married to a young hairdresser at Irene's salon and when the hairdresser is killed, Irene and Barry head back to the house to get to the bottom of things. Barry ventures in alone and we hear to gunshots. Irene rushes in to find out what's happened and ventures to the once-locked room. She finds her husband coming toward her, pushing her nearer to the gaping hole and to her imminent death. The man removes a mask to reveal that it is actually Barry, the lawyer.

Barry apparently rewrote the husband's will with him as the beneficiary and decided to drive Irene mad or kill her, whichever came first. But before he can do her in, the detective arrives and shoots Barry and we find that he and Barry were working together to split the fortune, but Barry decided to do away with the detective and his wife and take the money himself. The detective then decides to do away with poor Irene, but before he can, Barry rises and attacks him. In the scuffle the two men fall though the hole in the floor to their deaths and Irene is left to collect the inheritance and hopefully in time to get a good night's sleep.

The director of photography for the film was Harold Stine. It was actually Taylor who suggested him for the position after the two worked together on the 1964 film *A House in Not a Home*. "I was practically hired by telephone," said Stine.

Stine said he met with Stanwyck and she even agreed to shoots some tests before actual production began so the two would be comfortable working together. "She was most cooperative," he said. "She gave me the feeling that she was working for me."

Stine said they got along well during filming and reports say production took place without any major problems. Castle said the entire crew loved working with Stanwyck and affectionately called her "Missy."

"I used to watch in amazement as the electricians, high up in the rafters, shouted down, 'Hi, Missy!' She would look up and shout back with warmth," Castle once recalled.

For the first day of filming, Castle even invited the entire Hollywood press corps to watch. A scene in which the two stars discuss romance at a table for two in a small restaurant was their first scene together. While the romantic sequence could have been awkward for the stars, Taylor broke the ice by saying the restaurant reminded him of a little place the couple ate at in Chicago. Stanwyck agreed, jokingly recalling, "We ate ourselves out of shape there!"

Castle treasured the chance to work with Stanwyck. "In our work—I felt we were simpatico—something I rarely experienced with an actress, and I have worked with the best. It is a privilege to say I knew, loved and directed Barbara Stanwyck."

As for Taylor, when the press asked him how it was working with his ex-wife he replied, "It's as if we were never married."

The picture came together quite well and in reality, very little gore was added to the picture, making it somewhat of a departure for Castle from his standard horror. Stanwyck herself said one of the reasons she agreed to the film was because it was "a shocker suspense story...not a horror film."

Stanwyck's biggest problem was the fact that she had to scream continuously throughout the feature. But for Taylor it was slightly more difficult than playing the bad guy disguised as a good guy. Taylor was actually suffering from lung cancer after years of smoking. He would live for several more years, but some reports had focused on his poor health and its reflection in his appearance on screen.

In addition to Stanwyck, Taylor and Lloyd Bochner, other cast members included Hayden Rorke, Judith Meredith and Rochelle Hudson.

Hudson was back again with Castle after having worked with him on
the set of *Strait-Jacket*. Actor Hayden Rorke was hidden behind hideous
makeup for the feature, but would be better known to audiences for his
role of psychiatrist on the hit TV series *I Dream of Jeannie*.

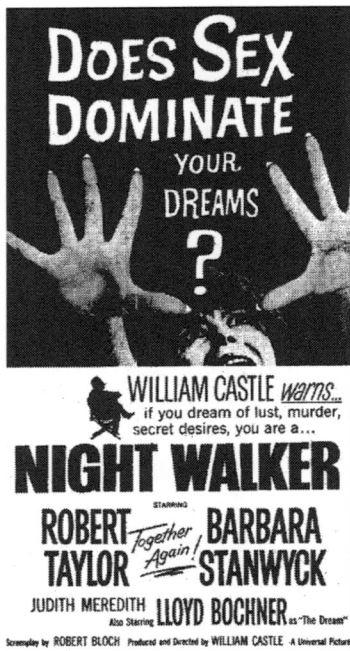

Sex was used to promote 'The Night Walker' in 1965 newspaper ads.

The Release

The Night Walker was released in January 1965 and a premiere party
was held by Universal Pictures and William Castle. Both Stanywck and
Taylor posed for photographs and when the picture showed up around

the country, Stanwyck did her bit, taking part in a promotional tour to draw fans to the theater. And while *The Night Walker* can hardly be called a smash it did return profits to Universal, Castle and its two leading stars.

Castle again went all out to promote the film. Advertisements promoted more eroticism with this feature. "Does sex dominate your dreams?" asked one ad. "William Castle warns if you dream of lust, murder, secret desires, you are a 'Night Walker,'" concluded the ad. Another ad warned viewers to not see the film if they were "afraid of things that can come out of your dreams…lust, murder, secret desires."

Theater owners were provided with posters, blowups, cutouts, luminous paint letters and other artwork to decorate the entire front of the theater to promote the film and he even gave them drawings and instructions to do it.

Reviews centered on Stanwyck for carrying the picture. Her performance was called "highly emotional" and "excellent." But the overall reviews for the picture were mediocre at best.

The New York Times critic Bosley Crowther wrote, "Some women crave furs and diamonds. Some crave love. But the woman who is the central character in William Castle's *The Night Walker* only craves a good night's sleep….This is the kind of eerie nonsense Mr. Castle is trafficking, with this latest of his calculated chillers…the whole thing would not be worth reporting if it didn't have Barbara Stanwyck in the role of the somnambulistic sufferer and Robert Taylor as her husband's lawyer who tries to help."

The writer called her performance "seasoned" and said it lends "an air of dignity" to an unbelievable tale.

The Night Walker was Barbara Stanwyck's last big screen performance. She reportedly received a number of film scripts, all in the horror genre after the film. She turned them all down saying she was tired being offered roles of "grandmothers who eat their children." Although

she continued performing on television in successful series, films and
miniseries, she would never again make a feature film.

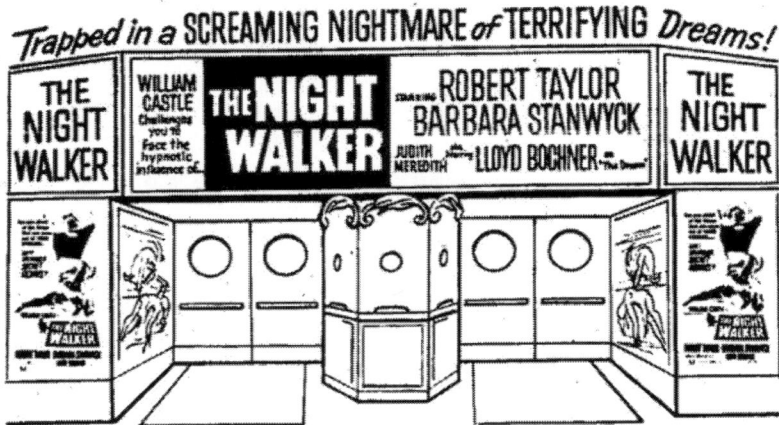

MAKE FULL USE OF YOUR ENTIRE THEATRE FRONT TO BILLBOARD
THE SHOWING OF "THE NIGHT WALKER." WITH THE EFFECTIVE USE
OF THE POSTER PAPER, BLOWUPS, CUTOUTS, LUMINOUS PAINT
LETTERING, LIGHTING AND ART WORK.

The above sketch is a suggestion for your front. Use the 3-sheets, 1-sheet, etc., on a front
panel with the strong catch-lines and scene stills effectively spotted in the inner side panels.
Complete the eerie shock and nightmarish dream effects with lighting and shadowing.

*For 'The Night Walker,' Castle provide theater owners with instructions
for decorating the theater to promote his 1965 thriller.*

Seeing Is Believing

Following on the heels of *The Night Walker*, Castle released another picture in the summer of 1965. This time the script was strictly aimed at the teen-age market, but Castle didn't want to mess with a good thing and decided a star name wouldn't hurt.

I Saw What You Did is based on a novel by Ursula Curtiss. It tells the story of a pair of girls who get in over their heads by making crank telephone calls to numbers in the phone book and telling the person at the other end, "I know who you are and I saw what you did." The game provides a humorous pastime until the girls use the title line on a killer who then sets out on finding them and doing them in.

The Casting

Castle purchased the film rights for the story and hired William McGivern to write the screenplay. In the roles of the girls he hired two unknown teen-agers who had never acted before. Andi Garrett and Sarah Lane were high school students the director chose for the film. Garrett played Libby Mannering, while Lane took the part of her friend Kit Austin. Libby's younger sister, Tess was played by Sharyl Locke. The role of the killer was handled by John Ireland and the parents of the children were portrayed by Leif Erickson and Pat Breslin. Breslin first worked with Castle for his 1961 thriller *Homicidal* and the film was also Erickson's second film with Castle, having starred in

Strait-Jacket. But they were not the only cast members with whom Castle had worked before.

Castle claimed that Universal allowed him to cast the unknown actresses in the lead roles if he could get a star in a cameo role. He immediately called Joan Crawford. Castle said he asked the star to do the role as a favor to him and she graciously agreed. However, there's actually a little more to the story.

Reports say that Crawford agreed to take the small role at her same salary as *Strait-Jacket*—$50,000. Castle agreed. Then Castle reportedly started a rumor that Crawford was put into the role and killed off early simply because he could not afford her. This also enabled Castle to use Crawford as the star of the picture even though she actually only appears on screen for a short time and in only a few scenes. It also allowed Crawford to retain her star billing and status for such a relatively small part.

Even with her name above the title, the role, like *Strait-Jacket*, was somewhat of a step down for Joan Crawford, noted director George Cukor, longtime Crawford friend. "Of course she rationalized what she did," said Cukor. "She would write to me about these pictures, actually believing that they were quality scripts. You could never tell her that they were garbage. She was a star, and this was her next picture."

The Production

Crawford had worked with costar John Ireland more than a decade earlier in her film *Queen Bee* and it would be familiar ground starring opposite him again. Castle himself claimed that the telephone was the actual star of the picture.

To get the young stars prepared for their roles the director said he allowed them to make some calls themselves. "I allowed them to actually make several crank calls a day from numbers picked at random out of the phone book. To experience the actual results, they improvised the calls, getting a sense of reality which they would later translate to the screen."

Castle had worked his formula into a finely-tuned machine. His horror films were crafted with certain elements in to provide the shocks, twists and turns needed to keep the story rolling along until the climactic finale. *I Saw What You Did* had all the elements of a Castle picture and in many ways was the culmination of his years in Hollywood.

A catchy, cute 60s pop-music theme begins the motion picture as Libby, on a split screen, calls Kit asking her to come over because her parents are going out of town for the night. The title and credits roll and then the film begins with the girls receiving instruction from Libby's parents who agree to leave even after the baby sitter cancels on them. Since the girls are teen-agers, the Mannerings figure they can care for Libby's younger sister Tess and the couple heads off for the night. After a tour of the house the girls begin playing telephone games and come across Steve Marak, a man who is about to murder his wife. When the wife, played by Joyce Meadows, enters the bathroom to tell him a girl is on the phone he grabs her, pulls her into the shower, and stabs her to death. Similar to Alfred Hitchcock's *Psycho*, the scene features the graphic details and blood. Then Castle puts on his touch by having Marak throw the fully-clothed woman through the glass shower door.

When Marak fails to get to the phone in time the girls hang up, but make a note of him and decide to call him back later.

The commotion causes a nosey neighbor, Amy, played by Joan Crawford, to venture in to see what's happened. Marak says he stumbled and gets rid of Amy, telling her his wife has left him. Steve Marak gets Amy out of the house and then disposes of his wife's body in a wooded area.

Amy, who has her sights set on Steve, returns to make a move for Marak and is upset when the girls call back and she thinks Steve has been having an affair. The girls whisper they know who he is and saw what he did and Marak believes they're onto him. He tries to keep the girls on the line to find out who they are, but they hang up. Amy, in the meantime, sees the bloody bathroom scene and realizes what Steve has done.

Later, the girls venture out to get a look at Steve after they copy his address out of the phone book. Steve catches a glimpse of Libby peering into his house, realizes who she is, and heads out to kill her. But before he can Libby is caught by Amy who shoves the girl away, telling her she's too young for Steve. Amy takes away the girl's car registration and sends her, and the other two girls who are hiding in the back seat, on their way. Amy returns to Steve telling him she got rid of the girl and plans to have him all to herself. She then tells him she's put two and two together and knows what's happened to his wife. Steve stabs Amy to death in a dramatic scene and uses the car registration to track the girls down to kill them before they can tell the police.

Kit's father picks her up and on the way home she hears about a murder on the radio and the killer fits Steve's description. When Steve shows up at the Mannering house, Libby convinces him she was only playing a prank, but then as he's leaving Kit calls and tells Libby about the murder and the girls realize what they've done. Before Libby can call the police Steve breaks in to kill her and a cat-and-mouse game ensues. As the movie reaches its climax Steve is about to do away with Libby and Tess when the police and Kit's father arrive and save the day.

John Ireland and Joan Crawford reunited onscreen for Castle's 1965 'I Saw What You Did.' The duo starred together first in 1955 in 'Queen Bee.'

In Need of a Gimmick

When asked why she decided to do the film, Crawford said at the time, "Because I think the film will have a terrific identity with parents and audiences." It's also likely that money was a strong selling point, because Crawford earned her $50,000 for a mere four days work.

Castle returned to his gimmicks for the release of *I Saw What You Did*. Castle decided that using the phone company for the promotion would be a good idea and arranged to have a phone number placed in ads around the country to promote the film. The ad asked people to call for a special message in which a young girl whispered "I saw what you did and I know who you are." The ad would then tell the listener to meet the girl for a date at the theater showing the picture. Castle also produced giant plastic phones to hang up outside the theater.

What Castle didn't expect is that his tag line became popular with local teens and the phone company began complaining that kids were tying up phone lines by making crank calls using his movie line. Castle said the phone company stopped allowing him to use phone numbers in his ads and removed his large plastic phones because they didn't want to be associated with the film.

Not one to give up, Castle devised a back-up gimmick that didn't use the phone lines. It was called the "Shock Section." Castle's "Shock Section" was the back three rows of seats in theaters which were equipped with seat belts, similar to those in airplanes. Once buckled in, moviegoers could view the movie without fear of shock jolting them from their seats.

Of all Castle's gimmicks this was considered the weakest. First, neither the studio nor the theater owners were willing to pay to have the seat belts installed on every seat in the theater, lessening the impact of the gimmick. Secondly, when used in conjunction with the film, viewers expected something on the screen that would shock them, and while the film was a horror and did have several killings, there were few genuine jolts, except at the very end when John Ireland's character jumps up from the back seat of the car to grab Libby who is sitting in the front seat. Moments later he is shot and killed by the police and the movie ends.

Castle did not appear in *I Saw What You Did* to offer any words of advice or introduction to his audience. In reality, he had not appeared his last few features. Having already established himself, there was no need to reinforce his image. The Castle trademark logo, by this point, began to appear on movie posters and promotional items for his films and that was possibly enough.

The Release

The film failed to create the interest many of his earlier films had and earned little attention at the box office. Reviews, while still far from glowing, did show that Castle had learned a thing or two over the years and directed a picture that some critics actually applauded.

Variety called *I Saw What You Did* a "well-produced, well-acted entry in the suspense-terror field," and added that Crawford's role "as Ireland's shrewish, predatory lover is well handled and vital to the story. Slightest gesture or expression of this veteran thesp conveys vivid emotion."

The New York Times said that the story had an "excellent" plot and called the child actors "altogether delightful," but added that the film was "a generally broad and belabored expansion of a nifty idea." Of the director, the reviewer wrote that the film could have been considerably better, "[U]nfortunately, William Castle, the director-producer, dawdles the tempo. And there is a redundant middle chapter involving the aroused, snarling killer, played by John Ireland, and his predatory, love-hungry neighbor, Miss Crawford."

The Saturday Review slammed the feature, saying "there is little for eye, ear, or mind in William Castle's egregiously low-budgeted *I Saw What You Did,* an attempt at terror starring Joan Crawford and John Ireland."

And the *New York Morning Telegraph* called it "another of those assembly-line shockers ground out with such regularity by producer William Castle."

After the release of *I Saw What You Did*, Castle began to see that the genre was no longer creating the stir it once had and even he could not create interest with his gimmicks and publicity stunts. "It was hard to believe that the low-budget exploitation picture was at an end," said Castle." Perhaps someday it would make a comeback, but I couldn't wait."

The Crumbling
of a Small Empire

By the mid-60s William Castle saw the writing on the wall and realized the genre of horror was on its way out. *Strait-Jacket* had been his only successful feature in a string of pictures that were, for the most part, panned by the critics and gimmicks that failed to draw in the fans. *The Nightwalker, I Saw What You Did, Zotz!, 13 Frightened Girls* and *The Old Dark House* all failed to meet the director-producer's expectations and he began to think the ride was over.

In an attempt to stay in the game Castle tried to steer away from the typical horror film and combine comedy, adventure and horror together and hope for the best. He had tried it in 1962 and '63, but found little success, but still Castle knew he need to expand his reach beyond horror to stay viable in the industry.

He felt that television was the cause of his troubles, as well as others in the industry. "Television was now becoming a formidable enemy of the movies," he said in his memoirs. "Business was off in theaters everywhere, and the sharp decline was starting to hurt me badly. In order to gain more revenue, movie companies had made the mistake of selling their almost current movies to television. As a result, people stayed home to watch free movies."

Castle's belief was well founded, but in addition, other factors came into play as well. Most studios were now in the business of television as much as in theatrical films. Universal, Castle's current home, in particular was finding much of its financial strength in the television market. Because of this the industry began producing fewer and fewer theatrical releases. And with profits down and fewer films being produced, the films that were made were often of a grand affair. Major studios were reluctant to fund small films like Castle's if they weren't drawing an audience. Instead, the studio would rather fund its television projects, which had a built-in audience.

Let's Kill Uncle

In 1965/66, Castle tried again with the production of another project called *Let's Kill Uncle*. Released in November 1966, the film starred Nigel Green, whose appearance as a traitor in *The Ipcress File* was used to promote Castle's latest feature, which was based on a novel by Rohan O'Grady. Mark Rodgers crafted the screenplay and the story takes place on a remote vacation isle where the young heir to a large fortune is being hunted by a professional killer. The boy and his island friend decide to get rid of the killer before he gets rid of them and there in lies the tale of adventure and suspense.

In addition to Green, the film starred Pat Cardi and Mary Badham in the roles of the children and Castle infused humor into the story as well to keep the tension from becoming too great. To create suspense the story avoided letting any of the other adult characters in the picture know the truth behind the killer's plot and the dangerous scenes include a deadly cliff, a deserted hotel, a tarantula, and a swimming pool filled with sharks.

Even with all the elements the film failed to garner much interest at the box office. However, Castle did receive some positive notice in the area of reviews when *The New York Times* wrote, "Say this for *Let's Kill Uncle*. It's the least bad chiller ever made by William Castle, whose specialty is usually buckets of gore on a low budget."

The review called it "certainly the best plot he has worked with in years" and applauded the children, calling them "quite nice" and adding, "Even Uncle has his points."

The Spirit Is Willing

Based on the novel *The Visitors* by Nathaniel Benchley, Castle decided his next picture would be called *The Spirit is Willing* and hired Ben Starr to craft the screenplay. Benchley, interestingly enough, was the father of Peter Benchley who went on to his own horror fame as the author of *Jaws*. The older Benchley had several films to his credit by 1967, including *The Russians Are Coming! The Russians Are Coming!* in 1966 and *Sail A Crooked Ship* in 1961. Starr, who would go on to work with Castle again for *They Busy Body*, had *Our Man Flint* (1965) and *The Pad and How to Use It* (1966), among others, to his credit.

The Spirit is Willing tells the tale of a couple and their teen-age son who rent a house by the sea in picturesque New England. They end up on a hunt for ghosts during the summer vacation when we learn that a woman once killed her bridegroom and his sweetheart in the house. The comedy adventure spun in a bit of horror and starred Sid Caesar, John Astin, Cass Daley, Barry Gordon and John McGiver and Mary Wickes. In addition, once again Castle followed Alfred Hitchcock and cast Vera Miles, one of the stars of *Psycho*, in his latest feature.

Released in early 1967, *The Spirit is Willing* also sank at the box office, but Castle didn't give up and had star Sid Caesar on board for another film.

Sid Caesar starred in two Castle features, 'The Spirit is Willing' and 'The Busy Body' both released in 1967.

The Busy Body

Sid Caesar had a long and successful career before he ever came in contact with William Castle. His greatest fame came in television in the 1950s and by the 1960s he was one of the most recognized entertainers in the world. His career in film was sporadic, but by the latter part of the 60s troubles with depression, in addition to drug and alcohol problems, caused his career to suffer. Castle's film projects provided Caesar an opportunity to work, a paycheck and a chance to stay in front of his fans. But in terms of furthering his career, the films did little.

The Busy Body followed quickly on the heels of *The Spirit is Willing*. In addition to Caesar, the film brought together a grand collection of comedians including Marty Ingels, George Jessel, Kay Medford, Jan Murray, Dom Deluise, Bill Dana and Richard Pryor, among others. Also starring in the picture were Anne Baxter and Robert Ryan. Sonny and Cher had cameo appearances as well.

In the feature Caesar plays a man who is characterized as an "overgrown mama's boy" who gets mixed up in a bum murder wrap and a collection of bumbling gangsters. Caesar is ordered to dig up the body of a man to recover $1 million which was apparently buried with him. The search for the missing million results in a madcap chase. Cameo comedic appearances provide much of the humor that made the film work.

Caesar recalled years later that he did the Castle films even though he knew they were "inane." "I didn't care," he said. He noted that his drug problems took a great toll on him and he was "barely aware" of the existence of his costars on the set. He was apparently forgiven by his fans and the critics. One critic said that his talents were wasted in *The Busy Body*. Caesar admitted that it wasn't that the projects were wasting his talents, it was that his "talents were on hiatus."

Once again, however, the film managed some worthwhile reviews from the critics when it was released in June 1967. *The New York Times* said the comedic cameos worked "pretty well" in the comic whodunnit because Castle "for once has played the macabre for laughs." The review went on to say that, "Much of the dialogue and gags are funny indeed."

Even with the reviews, though, the film could not be saved at the box office and once again, Castle was looking back at a string of failures, much as he had five years earlier. "My small empire was beginning to collapse," Castle admitted in his memoirs. He felt that he had tried everything and found it hard to believe his brand of horror was no longer interesting to the public. In New Orleans to promote the release of the picture, he admitted to one reporter, "I feel that the market for the horror film is past. It's had its cycle. Now I'd like to try something else."

He began looking for a project that would offer him a new direction, but found the process difficult. "Desperately, I started to search for the miracle that would save my career. I had to find something—anything—or I'd be out of business," he realized. But once again, just around the corner, the horror genre was about give him another boost.

Birthin' Satan's Baby

After years of directing, producing and promoting his cinematic creations, Castle's niche of creating campy horror was starting to wear thin. He no longer received the interest in his films they way he had a decade before and it had been several years since his last hit. Gimmicks weren't enough and the fans who he sought as teenagers had grown up into a world where horror wasn't such a stranger anymore.

In the decade since Castle emerged on the horror scene, a lot had happened. The country had watched in horror as President Kennedy was gunned down in Dallas and stood in shock at the images of his flagged-draped coffin. Leaders like Martin Luther King and Robert Kennedy were being assassinated in full public view. A war in Vietnam and a war at home in the form of a civil rights revolution had scared the public enough. Horror was something much more real now and seemed somewhat less palatable for the movie-going public.

Escape films had become the rage. *The Sound of Music, Doctor Doolittle, My Fair Lady* and *Doctor Shivago* were garnering attention and box office dollars, while horror films were no longer in fashion. Castle knew this and struggled in finding his direction for the future. His last few films had been attempts at new genres, but didn't receive much attention and left the fans he did have wanting more. He had directed himself into a corner and audiences expected horror in a William Castle film and if they had decided they didn't want to see horror. That also meant they didn't want to see William Castle. But could the right movie turn it all around. Possibly, Castle hoped.

In 1967, Castle received galley proofs of *Rosemary's Baby* from literary agent Marvin Birdt, but Castle had no intention of even reading the book, let alone making the movie. "You know the bottom has fallen out of horror films," Castle told Birdt.

"They'll knock you on your ass," replied Birdt of the proofs.

Castle agreed to read to proofs at home that evening and finished them in three hours knowing he had to make the movie.

The asking price to purchase the rights to the book was a quarter of a million dollars and Castle didn't have that sort of money. He wanted to think about it, but was told he'd better act fast because someone else was interested in it. The other person was rumored to be Alfred Hitchcock.

Castle had been a watching Hitchcock for years, but for all his effort he never received the acclaim that Hitchcock had. Castle knew *Rosemary's Baby* was his chance to shine.

Hitchcock supposedly turned down the film rights, but Castle on the other hand offered $100,000 in cash and five percent of 100 percent of the profits. And if the book became a bestseller, Castle promised an additional $50,000. Twenty-four hours later his deal was accepted.

Castle had planned to direct the movie, but Paramount Studios, who negotiated to film the horror, had another idea. They offered him $250,000 and 50 percent of the profits to produce the film. But for direction, Paramount had someone else in mind.

"Have you ever heard of Roman Polanski?" asked Charles Bluhdorn, one of the head executives at Paramount.

The studio was prepared to make a major motion picture out of the Ira Levin novel, but the production was something of a risk. First, horror was not doing much at the box office and since Castle's recent works had done poorly, it would seem that Paramount wasn't prepared to risk its money on another Castle horror picture—certainly not a big budget A picture.

"Of course," answered Castle, who knew of Polanski's flair for film-making and his early classics like *Knife in the Water*.

"If Polanski, with his youth, directed *Rosemary's Baby*, and you, with your experience, produced. You could teach each other so much," said Bluhdorn.

"No deal," said Castle.

But in time, Castle agreed to meet Polanski and found his ideas about the film suitable to his own. Castle bowed to Paramount and Polanski would direct the film. Polanski then adapted the screenplay and set forth to film the movie. His salary was only $150,000 with no net of the proceeds.

Much to Castle's displeasure, Paramount Pictures selected Roman Polanski to direct Rosemary's Baby, while Castle was left with the producing responsibilities only.

Producing a Classic

Castle must have resented the directing duties being passed on to another director, especially one without nearly the length of experience he had. However, Castle knew his last few films had done poorly and he felt the days of his brand of horror were over. He wasn't prepared to risk producing the film himself in order to direct it, and couldn't afford to, so Paramount's offer was quite appealing financially.

When it came to casting the role of Rosemary, Castle won out. Polanski wanted Tuesday Weld for the lead role, while Castle saw Mia Farrow. Robert Redford was chosen for the role of Rosemary's husband, but because of legal troubles with Paramount he was dropped from consideration. Jack Nicholson was reportedly interested in the role for a time, but John Cassavetes eventually was chosen for the part three days before shooting was to begin. And for the neighbors, Minnie and Roman Castevet, Ruth Gordan and Sidney Blackmer were chosen. Once the rest of the casting was rounded out production began.

Troubles on the set began almost immediately after production began in the fall of 1967, according to Castle. Polanski was known as a perfectionist, claimed Castle, and in the first six hours of shooting not a single shot was captured. "I was amazed at Roman's eye for detail," said Castle in his autobiography. "A perfectionist, he refused to compromise. If I had been directing the picture, I could have finished the scene in several hours. Polanski was taking several nights."

In another slow process, Polanski set the story in 1965 and insisted that every furnishing and item of clothing match the year. And while it was only two years earlier, the process became cumbersome.

The crew fell days behind schedule and Castle feared Paramount might shut down production. He urged Polanski to speed up the process, but Polanski refused to bend. "Rosemary will be a blockbuster, but I will not compromise. You understand, don't you?" said Polanski.

The picture dragged on until it was weeks behind schedule. Polanski's location shooting in New York caused mob scenes as the public invaded the set in hopes of seeing the stars, stopping production. Polanski's eye for detail and accuracy had him refusing to film scenes on Hollywood sound stages and Castle was having a hard time keeping things under control.

Mia Farrow had recently married Frank Sinatra and Sinatra had planned to star with his wife in his next film. But because *Rosemary's Baby* was behind schedule, Farrow would never be finished before the next production began.

"Mia's supposed to start my picture on Monday. Will she be finished by then?" asked Sinatra on the phone to Castle, who was amazed to be talking to Sinatra, but knew he didn't have an answer that would please him.

"No, Frank, I'm afraid that's impossible. Even by working Saturdays, she'll be at least three weeks," replied Castle.

"Then I'm pulling her off your picture tomorrow," said Sinatra.

"That'll mean shutting us down, Frank."

"Sorry to do that to you, Bill, but there's no other choice."

But there was another choice. And it was Mia Farrow's. She decided she wanted to finish the picture and her marriage felt the blow. Rumors said Sinatra threatened to divorce her if she didn't walk off the picture. And when she didn't, the story goes that Sinatra sent his lawyers to Polanski's offices during filming to deliver her the divorce papers. The marriage didn't last the year.

Another problem on the set was a clash of personalities between Polanski and Cassavetes. Shouting matches between the director and his leading male star were said to be commonplace during filming and their dislike for each other only grew as production dragged on. And the fact that Cassavetes was a director made the conflict worse as each insulted the other's style and work.

One of the final issues to face during production was whether or not to show the evil child. "Roman, do we ever let the audience see the 'Baby'?" asked Castle.

According to the book the child had orange-red hair and eyes that were golden-yellow without any whites or irises in them and had vertical black slits for pupils.

Polanski and Castle reportedly discussed various options for creating the devil child. Including using cat's eyes, budding horns on its head, and a demonic tail.

"Do you think the audience will be expecting to see it?" asked Castle.

"Of course," said Polanski. "But I don't think we should ever let them."

"They'll feel cheated," replied Castle.

"On the contrary, Bill. Everyone will have their own personal image. If we show our version—no matter what we do—it'll spoil that illusion."

"I think we should at least photograph the cat's eyes," said Castle.

"I disagree. If I do my job right, people will actually believe they've seen the baby."

The child was never photographed and Polanski created the film within his vision. The production, at last, came to an end and the film was cut and everyone was sure they had a winner on their hands. And they were right.

John Cassavetes and Mia Farrow starred in 'Rosemary's Baby' in 1968. The film would be Castle's greatest success as a producer.

Castle Strikes Gold with a Major Hit

The film proved to be the success Paramount was looking for after its release in June 1968. Total cost of the production was reported at a mere $2.3 million. The film, in its original release took in more than $15 million in box-office receipts, becoming the 34th largest money-making film of the decade and one of Paramount's top five money-makers of the 60s, eventually grossing more than $30 million.

Critics were mixed about the film. Some felt Polanski pulled off a fantastic effort, while other were left less ecstatic. Reviewer for *The New York Times,* Vincent Canby wrote, "Mia Farrow is quite marvelous, pale, suffering, almost constantly on screen in a difficult role that requires her to be learning for almost two hours what the audience has guessed from the start....for most of its length the film has nothing to be excited about...nothing cumulative—to fill that time with suspense. But the good side of that is that you can see the movie, and like it, without risking terrors or nightmares."

As the box office receipts flowed in, so did the mail. Castle claimed in his autobiography that he received an average of 50 hate letters a day after the film's initial release. "I've received crank letters on my other pictures," he wrote. "but none like these."

"Bastard. Believer of Witchcraft. Worshiper at the Shrine of Satanism. My prediction is you will slowly rot during a long and painful illness which you have brought upon yourself," wrote one moviegoer. Other letters called him a Satan worshiper, a purveyor of evil and said his soul would "forever burn in hell."

He tossed them off knowing it was one of the costs of success and looked to his bright future knowing the hit picture would be leading to profits and an opportunity to have his pick of projects. But, in addition to the nasty letters, a number of religious groups publicly blasted the film urging the public to boycott the film. But the publicity only added to the appeal, drawing moviegoers to the theater to see what all the commotion was about.

It's even been reported that Castle fell back into his old ways for the release of *Rosemary's Baby* and succumbed to the desire for a gimmick. Some say in an attempt to promote the film, the producer hired people to actually picket the theaters to draw attention to the film and its Satanic theme. And while the movie worked, gimmick or not, it also cast a shadow over the producer and several others tied to the film. It was a shadow that Castle himself called a curse and resulted in much pain and agony.

III

The Decline

Life after the Baby

Rosemary's Baby wasn't the only feature William Castle released in 1968. Another film, *Project X*, made its way into neighborhood theaters that year, and once again, at the helm was producer/director William Castle.

Project X

Science fiction was a popular genre in the late 60s. As the U.S. space program grew closer to putting its first man on the moon the public's interest in space and worlds beyond Earth grew. In 1968, *2001: A Space Odyssey* was a big hit, as were *Planet of the Apes* and *Barbarella*, and all ventured into space and science fiction. Castle's effort got lost in the shuffle and lagged far behind the competition.

The film takes place in the year 2118 when an American agent, returning to the U.S., sends out a cryptic message that the West will be destroyed in 14 days. The agent, Hagen Arnold, has been injected with a serum that is designed to erase his memory if he is captured and tortured by the enemy.

He is found unconscious and it appears the serum was activated, erasing his secret knowledge of why the West has only 14 days before destruction. Scientists attempt to restore his memory. The attempts lead to more mystery and danger until it is revealed that Arnold has been injected with an ancient bacterial culture that makes him a living death bomb set to go off in 14 days. He has been designed to spread disease and death that will kill everyone.

The scientists consider a quarantine of everyone who has come in contact with him at this point because the 14 days are up. They figure they will each die off, infecting no one else and saving the world. In the end they realize that because Arnold was cryogenically frozen between when he delivered the cryptic message at the beginning of the film and when he was found, the disease was inert, giving the scientists more time to find a cure and save themselves and the world.

Starring in the feature were Christopher George, Henry Jones, Phillip E. Pine, Lee Delano, Robert Cleaves, Harold Gould and Sheila Bartold. Special effects sequences for *Project X* were done by Hanna-Barbera Productions, best known for their cartoons.

The story was based on novels by Leslie Davies and the screenplay was written by Edmund Morris. Castle chose to direct the feature himself and Paramount Pictures, the studio responsible for *Rosemary's Baby*, released the picture. The feature was the last film he directed in the 1960s. Without his brand of gimmickry and possibly because the film took him into an entirely new genre, *Project X* fared poorly at the box office and Castle's own success in *Rosemary's Baby* outshined even the director's interest in the film.

Post-Rosemary Troubles

Castle's next offer following the release of *Rosemary's Baby* in the summer of 1968 came in the form of a dark comedy. Neil Simon's *The Out of Towners* offered Castle a chance to move on. It would be a major departure for Castle and another mainstream, critical success could put him on the map of major motion pictures. The producer's job was offered to him and he wanted it. No sooner had he agreed to go to New York and settle the deal than he felt a pain in his groin.

He thought it was just indigestion and he'd be in New York by Monday, but it was not to be. The pain grew worse, nausea followed and the room began to spin. He blacked out. It was Halloween and they found him unconscious on the floor of his home when his wife and children returned from trick-or-treating.

At the hospital they found there was a blockage. He drank lots of fluids, but could not urinate. He couldn't feel his legs. In surgery they gave him a spinal and finally the blockage began to come free. After six days he was able to go home.

Then it happened again. Back in the hospital and more surgery. It was kidney stones the size of small rocks. He was home again in two weeks.

Then it happened again.

Then again.

More time in the hospital and more surgery. He began to believe the letters of hate and the curse of *Rosemary's Baby*. He feared it was going to kill him he said. "The story of *Rosemary's Baby* was happening in life. Witches, all of them, were casting their spell, and I was becoming one of the principal players."

While Castle was battling his own evils in the hospital, fate struck again.

Christopher Komeda, the composer of *Rosemary's Baby*, had a blood clot suddenly rupture in his brain while skiing. He was admitted to the same hospital as Castle. He was in a coma. A short time later, after he had been awarded a Golden Globe award as composer for the film, Komeda died.

Castle no longer could stand on his own. He began seeing the best urologists he could find searching for a cure. There was a stone causing the main obstruction. Castle could no longer handle the surgery and feared he was going to die.

The only alternative was sodium bicarbonate injections. They were painful, but they might dissolve the stone. Castle decided it was better than surgery and took the injections. They were given twice a day, every day and caused him to suffer high fevers. Weeks turned into months and it looked like surgery would have to follow. But finally the stone began to dissolve. Castle began to get well. He thought the curse had lifted.

Back when Roman Polanski agreed to direct *Rosemary's Baby* he needed a place to live in California after the filming was finished in New York and at least for the duration of the picture. Castle claims he agreed to help him find a home before filming began. Polanski wanted a place near the ocean. Polanski's fiancee, Sharon Tate, would be the one to decide on the place.

Castle found a home in Malibu, but later, deciding they wanted a larger home, Polanski and Tate moved to a place hidden at the end of a lonely winding road on Bel Air Hill in Benedict Canyon. The red-wood house was at 10050 Cielo Drive and had a large lawn, a swimming pool and a guest house. The owner was a Hollywood business manager who had leased the home to the son of Doris Day, Terry Melcher, who was living there with his girlfriend, actress Candice Bergen. Melcher was moving and decided to sublet the house. Tate loved the place and it was settled.

But Tate was not aware of Melcher's tie to a bizarre character named Charles Manson. It appears that Melcher, who was a Hollywood record producer, was being pestered by Manson for a record contract. Manson, who lived with Beach Boy Dennis Wilson for a time and developed some of his music contacts through him, considered himself a would-be musician and sent Melcher some recordings he had made. Melcher never took any interest in the tapes and ignored him. But Manson became bitter, even showing up at his home looking for the demo tapes he had sent.

When Manson arrived at 10050 Cielo Drive in August 1969 Tate's personal photographer Shahrokh Haiami answered the door but didn't recognize the name Melcher and turned Manson away. Tate appeared at the door as he was leaving and reportedly asked "Who was that guy?" Manson supposedly turned back and looked at Tate, then left the scene. He had no idea Melcher had moved.

Later that night Manson told his followers, "You're going out on Devil's business tonight," and sent them to 10050 Cielo Drive, telling them "No one must survive." Some stories suggest vengeance against Melcher led to the crime.

Four of Manson's "disciples," Tex Watson, Susan Atkins, Patricia Krenwikle and Linda Kasabian, arrived at the house. Steve Parent an 18-year-old friend of caretaker William Garretson was leaving the guest house about 12:18 a.m. when the killers arrived. He was shot and killed in his car, but no one heard the killing. Watson, Atkins and Krenwikle then entered the main house, with Kasabian keeping lookout outside. They confronted Voytek Frykowski, a friend of Polanski's who was staying at the house with his girlfriend, Abigail Folger, heir to the Folger coffee fortune. In addition to Frykowski and Folger, Jay Sebring, Hollywood hairdresser and one-time boyfriend to Sharon Tate was spending the night to keep Tate company while Polanski was in Europe on movie business. The four were herded into the living room and then stabbed and beaten to death. The word "PIG" was scrawled on the white floor of the living room in Tate's blood. Manson was not present at the killings, but was later convicted of the murders along with the others.

Manson and his followers continued their murder spree by killing Leno and Rosemary LaBianca in Los Feliz in another grizzly murder scene and ranch hand Donald Shea was also killed, but his body was not found until eight years later. Gary Hinman, a friend of the Manson tribe was also killed at his Topanga home weeks before the killing spree by another of Manson's followers.

The murders looked like a ritualistic killing but at first the Tate and LaBianca killings were not linked. Polanski was questioned by the police and for a time was a suspect in the killings. There were stories of drugs and black magic and the Satanic story behind *Rosemary's Baby* fueled rumors for months about the killings.

Castle saw the headlines and believed it was another part of a curse. And as the acclaim of his latest film came he no longer cared. Castle wrote: "Ironically, all my life I had yearned for the applause, approval and recognition from my peers; and when the awards were being passed out, I no longer cared. I was at home, very frightened of *Rosemary's Baby*, and still very ill.

The murders had all of Hollywood cloaked in fear. Frank Sinatra was said to be in hiding and Mia Farrow refused to attend Tate's funeral because it was reported she was afraid she would be next. Many stars beefed up security and began carrying guns and there were numerous offers of rewards for catching the killers.

Castle physically recovered from *Rosemary's Baby*, but while the *Out of Towners* might have given Castle new-found success and the acclaim he desired, what he called the curse of *Rosemary's Baby* cost him the opportunity and the film was made without him. Although he did make another film in 1968. It would be released in early 1969 and would be his final project of the decade.

Riot

Following *Rosemary's Baby*, Castle accepted the producing duties for another film, a drama entitled *Riot*.

Riot is a drama based on a novel by Frank Elli. Elli actually wrote the book while serving time in prison and the story, appropriately enough, centers on a prison riot and an attempted prison escape. Again, it was a Paramount production.

First published in 1966, the book sold some 250,000 copies before it was released in paperback in January 1968. The film rights were sold to Paramount for $13,000. The screenplay was written by James Poe and the studio selected Buzz Kulik, whose experience was predominantly in television, to direct the feature.

The feature was filmed at the Arizona State Penitentiary and starred Jim Brown, Gene Hackman, Ben Carruthers, Mike Kellin, Gerald

O'Loughlin and Clifford David. For realism, the crew actually used inmates from the prison in supporting roles and as extras.

Before filming, Castle and Kulik visited the prison to plan location shooting and Castle sent 200 copies of the book to the prison to be distributed so the staff and inmates knew the details of the project that would be filming there, Some 400 convicts were tested for the supporting roles and 80 were selected for filming. The inmates were paid the standard actor's guild salary.

Security was tight during filming and everyone was required to wear an identification badge and have security escorts throughout the facility. There was a strict rule that no gifts could be exchanged between the crew and the inmates. And Associate Producer Dona Holloway was not allowed on location shooting because women were not authorized inside the prison walls.

The premiere was held in December 1968 at the penitentiary and along with star Jim Brown and the executives from Paramount, 250 convicts attended the screening. Castle's illness apparently kept him away from the showing.

Riot did offer filmgoers some stark realism and a look at a world that is often hidden from public view. Reviews were marginal after its release in January 1969. *The New York Times* wrote, "*Riot* is not a great movie, but it is a respectable one" and reviewer Vincent Canby added that the film is "not the sort of movie I would go out of my way to see, but then, once in the theater, I didn't feel the need to bust out."

Time magazine felt the movie's violence was excessive, writing "Even in these bloody times, the violence in 'Riot' is rather extravagant."

The Seventies

The movie business had changed a great deal over the course of the 60s, and by the 1970s the Hollywood studio system was entirely gone. Directors and stars were no longer placed under contract and careers were not molded or controlled by the studio system.

This new liberation enabled a lot of new and young talent to find success in Hollywood without the confines of the past. But for many of the older players, people like William Castle, it was less comforting and made the future much less clear.

Castle produced no works during the first few years of the decade, but in 1972 he worked as the producer of a TV series for NBC entitled *Ghost Story*. The show took to the airwaves in the fall of 1972 with Sebastian Cabot as its host. Cabot portrayed Winston Essex, who ran a hotel which was constructed from his former mansion. Cabot exited the show in December 1972 and when the show resumed in January the name had changed to *Circle of Fear*.

Although the series only lasted a season, it was somewhat familiar ground for Castle. It was an anthology series of suspense stories in which guest stars each week were confronted with the world of the supernatural. Notable guest stars included Janet Leigh, better known for her *Psycho* fame. Other guest appearances came from Elizabeth Ashley, James Franciscus and Helen Hayes.

William Castle continued to work into the 1970s, with 'Bug' in 1975 as his last big screen feature. The director/producer died in 1977 at the age of 63.

Shanks

When the series ended in 1973, Castle moved back to the world of motion pictures and signed on to direct his first picture since *Project X* in 1968. Paramount Pictures produced and released *Shanks*, a film that combined elements of horror, comedy and drama and starred Marcel Marceau, one of the legendary artists of pantomime. It was William Castle's last effort as director.

Marceau was at the top of his craft by the early 70s and had even had some experience in the world of film. Influenced by the silent films of Charlie Chaplin, Marceau studied mime and acting in Paris and formed his own mime company. In the 1950s he found worldwide acclaim in his "mimodramas"—complete stories told through the art of mime. His fame led to work as a writer and a painter and several feature films. In 1968 he appeared in *Barbarella*.

Castle, on the other hand, was falling behind in the game. Not since 1968 had he produced a noteworthy film, and that picture, *Rosemary's Baby*, was directed by Roman Polanski. Polanski's popularity as a leading director skyrocketed after the success of the horror while Castle's barely had enough heat to light a candle. By the mid 1970s, Polanski was one of Paramount's top directors and was working on his latest picture, another classic called *Chinatown*.

When Marcel Marceau and Castle met in late 1973 to discuss the project at Castle's beach house in Malibu the director wondered if he had done the artist a disservice by inviting him to take part in one of his horror films. Marceau apparently was thrilled with the opportunity to reach a large audience through film and to have a starring role in a major motion picture. Marceau emphasized that he did not want to make a strictly horror picture. "We will not make a horror picture...this you must promise," said Marceau.

"I don't know, Marcel—I can't promise."

"Fantasy, yes, but horror, no," explained Marceau.

"But my audience expects a horror film from me," claimed Castle

"My audience doesn't," said Marceau.

Eventually the project was ironed out. Paramount provided a limited budget, giving Castle the directorial duties. Paramount was not about to offer a major budget to the risky project and Castle's own films, while occasionally successful, never had big budgets. In reality, the fact that his films were somewhat inexpensive to make was the only reason they returned a profit. Except for *Rosemary's Baby*, he never had a blockbuster.

Castle wrote in his memoirs that he was hesitant about returning to the role of director, but Marceau, he claimed, had convinced him it would be a fantastic project for him to do and that he would bow to Castle's direction and decisions. Castle agreed.

Written by Ranald Graham, the story detailed an aging scientist named Old Walker and his deaf mute assistant, Malcom Shanks, who are experimenting with bringing dead animals back to life. When the old man dies, the deaf mute brings him back to life by electrically rewiring his body, turning him into something along the line of a walking puppet. He also brings back several others who help him fight the evil forces, which come in the form of a motorcycle gang.

The story was somewhat of a grim fairy tale with Marceau taking on the key roles of Shanks and Old Walker. Others featured in the film were Cindy Eilbacher, Philippe Clay, Read Morgan, Lara Wing and William Castle made a cameo appearance.

A Demanding Star

Castle found working with Marceau difficult. He demanded that his costumes and wigs be made in Paris and then complained about the results asking that they be done again. Castle refused. The star also wanted to alter scenes that Castle had staged because he felt they would work better another way.

Castle recalled that the two began "an invisible tug-of-war" on the set. Castle did admit that Marceau's suggestions were sometimes helpful and insightful, but that he did not comprehend the tight budget they were under and the shooting schedule didn't allow for extensive reshooting of scenes that Marceau was unhappy with. Castle even began to doubt himself, thinking that he should let the legendary mime artist have his way.

The set was reportedly filled with visitors who were eager to see Marceau at work. Castle said producers, directors and actors from Paramount and other Hollywood studios were on hand each day to see the great mime at his best.

When the film was finished Marceau asked Castle if it would be as big a hit as *Rosemary's Baby*. "I doubt it, Marcel," he replied.

"We tried very hard. Didn't we?" asked Marceau.

"That we did, Marcel."

"We have made a great picture. A classic. It'll play forever," Marceau responded.

"I don't know, Marcel. You were great, but I think I might have failed you. Your world of mime and my world of horror may not mix. Only the audience will tell us."

Shanks failed miserably at the box office. Many critics panned the film, but applauded Marceau's performance. It received better treatment overseas. Steven North, a producer on the film said "[I]t could have been the lowest-grossing movie ever made by Paramount."

The star himself said *Shanks* "was difficult for its day. I played duel roles, and the film shifted from fantasy to reality without warning. It is a cult film in Europe though."

The New York Times said the teaming of Castle and Marceau made "a decidedly strange combination of talents. They and their company are as unusual as might be expected but they leave a viewer uncommitted, if not confused, by their largely far-out, somber fiction."

One interesting note is that they described Castle as the producer of such "spellbinding horrors as *Rosemary's Baby* and *House on Haunted Hill*," yet *Rosemary's Baby* only received a mediocre review from the film while *House on Haunted Hill* was panned by the paper when it was released.

The reviewer, A.H. Weiler said that Marceau failed to create the same magic he did on stage, but that his pantomimes were at times "strikingly charming."

One highlight of the feature was its score. Steven North, a producer on the film, helped pull in the talents of his father, Alex North, to write the music. Best known for his musical scores for A *Streetcar Names Desire, Who's Afraid of Virginia Woolf?, Spartacus, Cleopatra* and countless others, Alex North was well-respected in Hollywood and his work on *Shanks* earned him an Academy Award nomination for Best Music, Original Dramatic Score. North once said, "It was a thrill working with Marcel Marceau on *Shanks*, although no one saw the film."

The End of an Era

In December 1973 *The Exorcist* was released in the United States. It was a box office smash. It became the most successful horror picture to date and renewed interest in the genre that had seen little success since *Rosemary's Baby*, more than five years earlier.

Never one to pass up on an opportunity, William Castle wanted to ride the tailcoats of the genre once again in hopes of finding a hit. "I felt 1975 would be a big year for me if I could find the right material for a film," he wrote in his memoirs. He recalled hearing about other major pictures in production during that time, including *Earthquake, The Towering Inferno* and *Jaws*, and believed that it would be a frightening year at the movies and he needed to be a part of it.

Bug

"I had very little money to work with, and I knew I would be in competition with the multimillion-dollar disaster films the other studios were preparing," said Castle. He was still working with Paramount, as he had been since the late 1960s after the success of *Rosemary's Baby*. However, his track record was far from solid and the horrific response to *Shanks* only made his efforts more risky, but in 1974 he found a project and convinced the studio to distribute the film.

The film is based on Thomas Page's novel *The Hephaestus Plague* and Castle wrote the screenplay himself with the help of Page. He decided a name change was in order. Named after the Greek god of fire, Hephaestus, the title was acceptable for a book, but Castle knew it would never do for a film. He even said that during casting of the picture many of the actors who called about the film would get the name wrong, calling it "The Hepatitis Plague" or "The Hibiscus Plague."

Admitting that he personally liked one-word titles, he began searching for a proper name. *Macabre, Homicidal, Strait-Jacket, Riot* and *Shanks* had worked for him, and titles like *Jaws* and *Earthquake* were coming, so he wanted something easy to remember. He claimed his daughter Terry actually gave him the idea for the name when she yelled at her sister, "Don't bug me!"

Bug, he felt, was easy to remember, one word, and aptly described what the film would be about. Next he needed the proper creature.

Insects from Hell

Bug tells the story of a small town that, after hit by a strong earthquake, is invaded by large bugs that have lived for years deep inside the earth. Living on charred ash, the bugs are capable of starting fires and begin terrorizing the town.

Keeping costs down to a minimum Castle utilized the talents of many people who were working mainly in television. The director, Jeannot Szwarc, had most of his experience on the small screen, having directed shows like *The Rockford Files* and *Columbo*.

The stars of the picture also had strong experience in TV. Bradford Dillman began in film, winning a Golden Globe award in 1959 as most promising newcomer, but had transitioned into television with a variety of TV movie and series appearances on shows like *Columbo, Mission Impossible, The Night Gallery* and *Mary Tyler Moore*. Joanna Miles started in soap operas like *The Secret Storm, The Edge of Night* and *All My Children* and did a variety of other television projects over the years. Others in the cast included Alan Fudge, Richard Gilliland, Jamie Smith

Jackson and Patty McCormack, who was best remembered for her starring role in *The Bad Seed*, but also did television work.

But for Castle, the real stars of the film were the bugs and he went to great efforts to cast the perfect creatures.

Castle felt that audiences of the day were more sophisticated than in the 1950s and he couldn't use mechanical bugs or special effects, but needed the real thing to scare audiences. Someone suggested Ken Middleman, a director of photography at the University of California at Riverside. He had done insect photography for another film, *Hellstrom Chronicles,* and was recommended. Castle contacted him and he arranged to find the proper bugs which, Castle claimed, were trained for the film. Getting them to behave may have actually been easier that the actors.

Castle explained in his memoirs that much of the cast and crew were afraid of the bugs and didn't want them crawling on them. Fake bugs were used in some of the scenes with the actors.

Not all scenes made it into the final picture. Castle wrote in his memoirs that MPAA ratings board complained about one of his scenes in which bugs chew an actress' head off and it then rolls onto the kitchen floor. Castle thought teen-agers would love the gore, but the scene never found its way into the movie.

For the final scene, large flying insects were expected to pour from a crack in the earth. Castle couldn't find a bug with red wings that was large enough to create the menacing feel he was hoping for. Middleman managed to make the scene work by shooing common flies with phosphorescent powder on their wings to make them look red. Special effects were used to enlarge the flies so they looked much bigger and Castle was happy with the resulting scene.

The movie begins with James Parmiter, a university scientist, dropping his wife off at church. He leaves for work and she heads to mass when a severe earthquake strikes and townspeople run for cover. Large bugs are released through a huge crack in the earth and begin to menace the small town. They travel in car exhaust pipes because they live on ash and carbon. The bugs release fire from their bottoms and soon fires are exploding cars, setting houses and farms on fire and killing innocent bystanders.

A local student discovers the bugs and brings them to the attention of Parmiter who begins studying them. After his wife is killed by one of the nasty creatures he barricades himself in a small house and begins intense research. His study leads him to mate the bugs with a common cockroach and the bugs then begin reproducing. They also begin to show signs of intelligence, by crawling into formation and spelling out words on the wall like "We Live" and "Parmiter."

Eventually the bugs escape and crawl back into the earth, only to rebirth, but this time flying and finding their way into the house to kill Parmiter. The bugs somehow return to where they came from and another movement of the earth closes the crack, sealing them inside once again and saving the world.

Bug was released to dismal reviews and little box office. Castle, however, had one last gimmick up his sleeve in hopes of drawing some attention to his film. He mounted a large promotional tour for the premiere of *Bug* in a number of U.S. cities. On the tour he brought along one of the stars of the picture, a large bug named Hercules. His promotional gimmick traveled back to his 1958 release of *Macabre* and this time, instead of insuring the audience against death, he insured his bug to the tune of $1 million. If the bug was to die of natural causes during the promotional tour, excluding any unnatural or violent death, Castle would receive the money.

It was one last publicity stunt, but it didn't help the movie. *Bug* earned terrible reviews and, as Castle had feared, the film found it difficult to compete at the box office among the big budget features released in 1975. While some reviews called the film "weird" and "undeniably stupid," the *New York Times* went a step further when it said "It is not simply a scary picture, nor simply a violent one. It is a cruel picture."

The review went on to say the film "does vile things," and "is sick, and literally sickening." It urged viewers to not go see the movie and analogized it by saying, "If a restaurant reviewer eats a poor meal, that's one thing. If he gets ptomaine poisoning, that's another. *Bug* is decidedly poisonous."

Stephen Farber, another *New York Times* writer, wrote a blistering criticism of *Jaws* in its release that same year and compared both films. "Both *Jaws* and *Bug* belong to the Pavlov dog school of filmmaking," wroter Farber. "They treat the audience like laboratory animals wired to twitch whenever the electricity is turned on."

But Farber added that while *Bug* was easily recognized as a "cheap exploitation picture" the Steven Spielberg film was an "$8 million exploitation picture."

For Castle, any comparison to the smash horror hit was probably the best he could have hoped for.

Back to His Roots

Having started as an actor on the stage approximately 45 years earlier, Castle returned to acting in 1975 and 1976 with two small roles. He had been at Paramount since 1966/67 and in the nearly ten years there had established relationships and contacts with many on the lot. In addition, his talents before the camera had proved useful for several small screen appearances in his later films like *Rosemary's Baby* and *Shanks*. He accepted a role in an ABC television movie called *The Sex Symbol* in 1974. And his onscreen introductions for his own productions were well known, so Castle's time before the cameras had been well established.

In 1975 he accepted a small role as a movie director in John Schlesinger's film *Day of the Locust*. That role was followed by an offer to appear as a producer in Hal Ashby's *Shampoo*. *Shampoo*, starring Warren Beatty and Goldie Hawn was a huge hit, and although Castle's role was small, he finished his career as a professional actor with a part in a major motion picture.

In addition, in 1974 and 1975, Castle wrote his memoirs discussing his early years in the business and his climb to the post of King of the Gimmicks. Published in 1976 by Putnam Publishing, his memoirs were aptly titled, *Step Right Up! I'm Gonna Scare the Pants off America.* He dedicated the book to his wife and children and to all the kids he had scared over the years.

The Death of William Castle

Castle continued to search for appropriate projects in his last few years. Following the release of *Bug,* Castle considered several projects. One script, written by newcomers Kathy Gori and Alan Berger was entitled "Last Rites." The story was a thriller set at a Roman Catholic boarding school. Castle reportedly didn't want to produce the film, but was impressed enough with the writers to ask them to develop another story based on the concept of life after death.

In the meantime, Castle found another project called *200 Lakeview Drive.* The film was for MGM and was described as "a contemporary suspense drama which takes place in the world's most elegant high-rise apartment complex."

However, on Tuesday evening, May 31, 1977, William Castle suffered a heart attack at his home in Beverly Hills. He was taken to the University of California at Los Angeles Medical Center where he was pronounced dead later that evening. He was 63 years old. He never finished his final production and ironically, his project under development about life after death was never finished.

Funeral services were arranged by his family and held on June 3 in Hollywood. His obituary in *The New York Times* highlighted his greatest success as *Rosemary's Baby* and detailed his low-budget horror successes of the 50s and 60s. Castle was quoted from a 1960 interview he gave, saying, "I modeled my career on (P.T.) Barnum. Exploitation is the big thing in the picture business today. Stars and contents don't mean much at the box office anymore. The people who go to see pictures because of what's in 'em, they're a minority. Gimmicks, surprise, shock—that's what draws the crowds."

IV

Analysis

A Career in Retrospect

When William Castle died in 1977 he left behind a motion picture legacy—not necessarily the illustrious legacy he might have hoped for when he set foot inside Columbia Pictures in 1939, but a legacy nonetheless.

As a director he never achieved the level of success of those he admired most. Directors like Frank Capra, George Stevens, Orson Welles, and perhaps most of all, Alfred Hitchcock, earned honor and acclaim for their cinematic works. Castle, though, earned the wrath of critics who were either annoyed at having to see his movies, let alone write about them, or those who delighted in the opportunity to once again criticize his work and his chosen career.

But Castle refused to make movies for the critics, he made them for his fans. And they accepted him. When they stepped into the theater they knew what was in store and they often enjoyed the ride.

In time, those same critics who tore into him also began to expect a William Castle picture before they viewed the film and their reviews actually began to judge him on his own scale. And, as the public grew tired of his horrors and his gimmicks, the critics had finally caught on and actually reviewed the films more favorably than his major hits. Box office failures like *Let's Kill Uncle* and *The Busy Body* earned stronger reviews than *Macabre, House on Haunted Hill* and *The Tingler*, yet today, those early films are the highlights of his career.

An Analysis

To gain a better understanding of William Castle and his cinematic contributions it's important to take several factors into consideration. The times in which he worked and lived help explain his cinematic intentions. And in the years since, his body of work has influenced a generation of movie-makers and players in the world of horror. And while there are no attempts here to elevate Castle into a class he didn't belong, it is possible, after some analysis, to develop respect for what he was trying to accomplish.

While he has never been placed alongside Alfred Hitchcock, Orson Welles and countless others A-picture directors he admired, he can't be simply categorized among the mass of B-movie directors of his era. In reality, he stands somewhere between the two groups, in a place all his own.

The first important consideration is to understand where the director had come from. By the mid-1950s William Castle was longing for a place for himself. While other major directors were controlling their futures through the projects they selected, Castle was deep in the world of the studio system. He had been there for years. Since 1939, and his first contract at Columbia, Castle was expected to tow the studio line. At first it was whatever was asked of him—acting, writing, editing and eventually directing projects that were handed to him.

As a director he was given B picture after B picture. Shuffling the productions through while keeping them within schedule and on budget was all that was expected. There would be no Academy Awards, no elevation to A pictures, and certainly no share of the profits of his pictures. Actor Robert Mitchum once said that if you worked hard under the studio system and did well, you didn't get better, you got more. This was true for William Castle. And even though this may have been common practice in Hollywood, Castle wanted better.

Directors he admired had control over the projects they chose, even within the confines of their contracts they could select pictures they believed in. Many chose pictures that had a message to deliver or films that would challenge them and the industry to do bigger and better films. Epics, all-star casts, and new processes that had never been tried before were used to set directors and studios apart. Castle, though, and most of his B-movie counterparts, continued mass production of average films—the films that gave the "quality" pictures something to rise above.

For Castle, by the mid 50s he simply wanted to select projects he would enjoy and films he saw had a chance of setting him apart from the pack. He knew how to make the films, but didn't have the clout or the money to compete with the Hitchcocks of Hollywood, so he found projects he enjoyed producing and directing that he also knew he could sell to a market. And selling was key factor. Castle certainly never hid the fact that he was in the business to make money and his films were aimed at commercial audiences and not critics.

Horror and suspense were elements he himself had long loved and the teen market was eager to pay for whatever Hollywood could come up with. His gimmicks were only the extra push he needed to get his product in front of the public and away from the countless others pictures he was competing against. He wasn't trying to send a message through the films he produced and directed, but attempting to enjoy his work and make a profit at the same time.

The 1950s

Understanding the climate of the world in the 1950s helps explain the success of Castle and his films. To simply write him off as a mediocre talent fails to address the fact that although his talents as a director were far from those of the leading directors of his era, his was a style somewhat new to the moviegoing public and in many ways was a product of the environment.

David Skal, author of *The Monster Show*, explained in his book that the 1950s saw a shift in the style of horror. Since the early days of the film industry, monsters like Frankenstein and Dracula provided the staple of our fears, and the battle was often as basic as good vs. evil as man combated the beast. With the advent of the 1950s, the monsters of yesteryear were no longer compelling to the public and Hollywood began exploring other forms of fear. Following World War II, fear of mass destruction and nuclear war were real and provided new avenues for horror film as film explored the most basic elements of the danger that loomed in the back of our collective consciousness.

During this period, horror films consisted mainly of monsters and the monsters began to evolve into two distinct groups. The first, giant mutations came from the unknowns surrounding atomic testing. Taking things that were relatively harmless in their usual form and mutating them from massive doses of radiation into giant monsters caught the public's interest. Giant spiders, ants, lizards, squids and countless other images became popular horror villains.

The second horrific threat came in the form of aliens from other worlds. Space and the unknown provided us with new fears from outside our small planet. Invasions from Mars, flying saucers, body snatchers and more were fantastic images that gave us cause for alarm as man began exploring the world outside his Earth.

When William Castle came along in the latter part of the 1950s, his brand of horror turned inward at ourselves. The monsters were not from other worlds or freaks of nature, but from within. Men who buried children alive, murderous husbands, "Tinglers" inside us, and homicidal maniacs showed us that horror was closer to home and less easy to identify.

While this was not entirely unique, for Castle it became a horror format for the construction of most of his films. There were numerous features in the years before his foray into horror that carried similar elements. *Sorry Wrong Number* in 1948, *The Dark Mirror,* 1946, and *The Spiral Staircase,* also in 1946, were early ventures into the genre that succeeded, although none are considered authentic horror films, but drew more on suspense to promote the pictures. Castle combined these suspense elements with the more graphic elements of horror.

Even the films he imitated, like *Diabolique* and *Psycho*, were usually characterized as suspense or mystery dramas while Castle's features were categorized as strict horror. He adopted those horrific elements as the selling points for his films, letting the suspense, drama and mystery elements stay in the background. His films promised severed heads, vivid depictions of decapitation, and bathtubs full of blood. This direction was an attempt to cater specifically to the teen-age market. Other directors, like Hitchcock, for example, directed their films at a wider demographic crowd of moviegoers.

For Castle, the teen-age market became his bread and butter and it was this audience he spoke to when he introduced his films. It was a wise decision for several reasons. First, the youth of the 1950s were not often swayed by newspaper reviews that panned his films. They were interested in scares, gore and fun—elements reviewers often avoided in evaluating the worthiness of a movie.

Secondly, and probably most importantly, the teen-age movie audience was a huge market to tap. In 1958, when Castle debuted *Macabre*, audience members who were between the ages of 12 and 25 made up 72 percent of the movie-going public. Even prior to that, as is still the case today, the youth of America was the strongest demographic segment in theaters, but in the late 1950s it was even more so.

It was because of this market that horror films became so common. As mentioned earlier, in 1958, 75 horror films were produced and in 1959, as many as 100, accounting for 150 hours of entertainment, and earning a profit of roughly $100 million. "Thank god for horror pictures," said one manager of a large drive-in theater. "They saved us.

Before this kick we were thinking of shutting down two nights a week; now, with all the monster stuff, the place starts filling up at three o'clock. The kids go for it."

Interestingly enough, while the comment from the drive-in manager stood for the standard movie houses as well, the drive-in market was one market Castle had trouble selling to. This was simply because his gimmicks didn't work there. It was impossible to wire seats, fly skeletons overhead and use fright breaks with a drive-in audience. However, the gimmicks themselves were compelling enough to pull teens from their cars and into the theater to experience the sales promotions along with the movie.

Castle's gimmicks helped set him apart from the countless other horror pictures released during these key years, but he was not entirely alone. Hollywood had been using gimmicks for years in one form or another. CinemaScope, Cinerama, 3-D, VistaVision, Panavision, RegalScope, Camera 65, Technirama and SuperScope were all film processes that were marketed as new motion picture experiences. One process, Smell-o-Vision attempted to go where Castle had not gone, but was short-lived.

Even Howard Hughes jumped on the gimmick bandwagon in the mid-50s, premiering his film *Underwater*, starring Jayne Russell, actually underwater, suiting up reviewers in scuba gear for viewing the film.

For Castle, though, the gimmick did not start and end at the screen like the popular screen processes his names mimicked. Even Hughes' early effort for *Underwater* was only offered to the critics and he himself found out the hard way that they were not the ones to cater to. The critics panned his film and the public got just another black and white adventure yarn on water, which they quickly lost interest in.

With Castle's films the gimmicks were intended for the teen-ager sitting in the theater. Often, it was something tangible like an insurance policy, a Punishment Poll, or a Ghost-Viewer. They were the ones who paid the price of admission and Castle promised them something new and that was the reason they came.

Castle's brand of horror helped pave the road for things to come. And while Alfred Hitchcock is often credited with ushering in the new age of the horror film with the release of *Psycho* in 1960, Castle's films are in part responsible for that film. Castle was one of the few directors Hitchcock himself was attempting to copy when he made *Psycho*. Hitchcock had seen numerous low-budget features capitalize on his suspense style and decided that *Psycho* was his opportunity to make his own low-budget horror feature. The cycle continued when Castle made his own *Psycho*, releasing *Homicidal* in 1961. *Homicidal* became the first, and some say the best, of the *Psycho* imitations. What followed was a slew of horror films that elevated the body count and the gore, forever changing the horror landscape.

The Man in His Movies

Additional insight into the career of William Castle can be gained in reviewing the major body of his work, beginning with *Macabre* in 1958. By studying certain elements of these films we can see various traits of his personality emerge and understand that certain events in his life had a large impact on him and the films he created.

While it does not appear that Castle intentionally used imagery and themes to address his own issues and fears, it is apparent that on some conscious or subconscious level the director placed more of himself in his films than he may have been aware.

Alfred Hitchcock placed much of himself in his pictures, touching on his fear of police, his relationship with his mother, the death of his father and his own issues regarding his sexuality. In addition, his films contained themes, like the use of birds, and man's relationship with them, in his film *Psycho* and then the his follow-up film *The Birds*, which waged an all-out war between man and feathered foe.

Countless books have been written about Hitchcock and his films, many addressing the voluminous hidden themes within them and the reasons they were placed there. For William Castle this is not the case. Where Hitchcock was detailed and deeply involved in the process of filmmaking, Castle was not. Castle was eager to market his films and often spent little time planning and directing the productions. Intricate details were of little interest to him and it would not have been common

for him to have placed much thought in them or to devise hidden messages within his movies.

Castle did, however, play a great role in the formation of the stories
he told. He often gave the screenwriter specific details of the story and
the structure behind it, then allowing the writer to craft the dialogue
and scenes around the story. It's within these aspects of his motion pictures that we get a glimpse of the director himself.

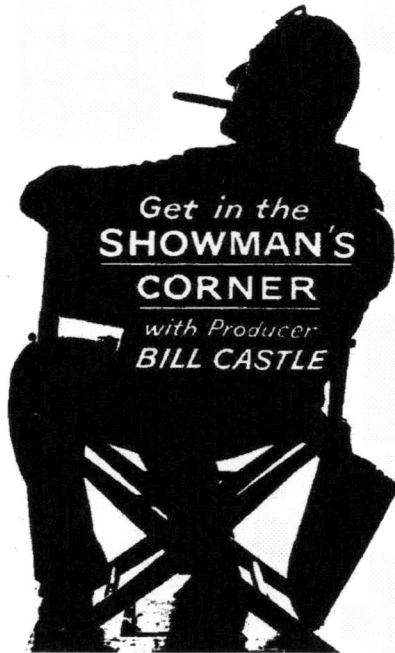

*Castle's logo, similar to Alfred Hitchcock's famous profile, became a
familiar sight on all Castle's movie posters, ads and other film
promotions. He also began introducing his films onscreen, similar to
Hitchcock's introductions in his popular TV series.*

The Loss off His Parents

It was at a very young age that William Castle lost both his parents. The effect this had on him must have been great, as it would have been on any child. The lack of a mother and a father during his childhood left him with very unhappy memories of those years and his memoirs offer vivid detail of his troubled youth and his feeling of worthlessness.

In viewing this within the context of his films, the lack of parental figures is evident in many of Castle's works. It's important to again note that for this discussion, Castle's real career as a director and producer began with *Macabre* in 1958. The features he made under the studio system would not have been given as personal a touch of the director because the stories were often written entirely by someone else. While these films are important in establishing his capabilities and style that affected his future films they fail to display any real picture of the man who made them.

In *Macabre*, the only child featured in the film is motherless at the beginning of the picture and by the end of the picture she is fatherless, leaving her alone in the world at the age of three.

Many of Castle's other films never identify the adults as parental figures of any kind. In *House on Haunted Hill*, no adult is ever identified as a parent. Nora, the youngest guest at the party, does have a family, however, in the film all the remaining members of her family were injured in a car crash and she is the only one who can support them financially, in effect making her responsible for herself.

In *The Tingler*, Doctor Chapin and his wife are left to care for his wife's younger sister after her parents have passed on. In *Homicidal*, Warren is raised by the nurse who helped deliver him after both his parents have died. *Mr. Sardonicus* is left disfigured after the death of his father and Joan Crawford's daughter in *Strait-Jacket* is left fatherless and motherless after her mother kills her father and goes off to an asylum for the insane for 20 years.

The wealth of the story in *I Saw What You Did* takes place as the parents are absent from the picture, abandonning the young girls who are left alone to deal with a dangerous killer. And *13 Frightened Girls* spent most of its time ignoring the question of whether the girls had parents or not as they were shipped off to boarding school and, in effect, were parentless. Even Castle's last film, *Bug*, which he wrote screenplay, has a teen-age daughter who watches her father die in a car explosion.

Inheritance

Another theme that wound its way through Castle's productions is the concept of inheritance. At the age of 25 Castle inherited a portion of his father's estate, picking up his first check for $10,000 on his 25th birthday. This event had a large impact on his entire career, for it was with these funds that he established himself in the world of the theater, and it was this path that led him to Hollywood and his future fame and fortune. But inheritance in his films most often came at a high price.

Inheritance is one of the most common factors linking his pictures together starting with *Macabre*. The intent behind the murderer in the 1958 film is to obtain a $10 million dollar inheritance. The doctor, whose daughter is feared buried alive through the entire picture, has devised the entire plot to scare his father-in-law to death so that he can inherit his vast fortune which would go to the doctor's young daughter. In the end of the picture, both the doctor and the father-in-law are dead leaving the money to the little girl who was never really buried at all.

For *House on Haunted Hill* the inheritance comes in the form of a $10,000 check to anyone who manages to spend an entire night in the haunted house. In the end, all the guests—except for the host's wife and her lover, who both die in a vat of acid—are alive to receive their money.

In *The Tingler*, Dr. Chapin's wife controls the purse strings of her parents' money after they have died. It is this money that enabled Chapin to study the beast of fear. Chapin's wife also controls her sister's share of the money, using it to prohibit her from marrying Chapin's assistant, a young man who will "ruin her sister's life" just as Chapin did to her by putting science before their marriage, she thinks.

In *13 Ghosts*, the entire story revolves around the inheritance of a large old haunted house from a recently-departed uncle. All the uncle's money is hidden in the house and the lawyer's motive is to use the ghosts to scare the family out of the house so he can find the money.

The theme behind *Homicidal* again involves a large inheritance when the young girl is disguised and raised as a boy so that she can inherit her father's fortune on her 21st birthday. And in *Mr. Sardonicus* the inheritance comes in the form of a lottery ticket that the son must reclaim from the pocket of his dead father's vest. He must dig up his father's body to obtain the ticket, causing him to be disfigured from the shock of seeing is father's rotting corpse.

For *The Old Dark House*, the plot revolves around a killer in the Femm family that is murdering the family members in order to obtain the entire family fortune. In *The Night Walker*, Barbara Stanwyck is due to inherit her blind husband's wealth, but the husband's lawyer has actually put his name in the will instead and concocts a plot to get rid of her so he can get his hands on the fortune. Inheritance and missing money also play a key roles in the story of *Let's Kill Uncle* and *The Busy Body*.

Locked Rooms

It may simply be the nature of the genre, but locked rooms are a familiar theme in Castle films. It's unclear that there is any real fear or personality issue addressed by these locked rooms, but many of them hold a secret to the films they are part of.

In *Macabre*, the locked room holds the truth that the doctor's daughter has never actually been buried, but is actually asleep in a small room at his medical offices. A key in his hand unlocks the door at the conclusion of the film as the nurse ventures inside to find the little girl alive and safe.

In *House on Haunted Hill* an apparently locked door separates Nora from Lance when the ghosts get between them and their safety is in danger. In addition, the guests are each urged to lock themselves in their rooms and wait out the night in the haunted house after all are locked inside the house with no way to escape after the caretakers leave for the evening.

Dr. Chapin, in *The Tingler*, locks himself inside his lab to test the effects of LSD on himself as his assistant and sister-in-law watch in horror through the small window in the door, unable to get in to help him. And a locked safe in the film holds the riches from the deaf mute woman's business.

A secret locked room is revealed as the rich uncle's laboratory in *13 Ghosts* and several hidden spots in the house reveal items like a Ouija board, a diary and the hidden money. In *Homicidal*, Emily uses a key hidden outside to gain entry into Miriam's locked flower shop so she can smash things up and vent her hatred for Miriam. In the end of the film, entry into the unknown horror of the house is drawn out by Castle's fright break which gives moviegoers an opportunity to leave the theater before Miriam ventures inside the dark house to discover the horror that awaits her.

The Night Walker uses a lock to keep Barbara Stanwyck from the room in which her husband was killed in an explosion. Stanwyck must venture into the locked room at the end of the film to uncover the secret behind her living nightmares.

Locked or closed rooms also hide secrets, most often dead bodies, in *Mr. Sardonicus, 13 Frightened Girls, Strait-Jacket* and *I Saw What You Did.*

The Independent Woman

One interesting factor in Castle's film is the role of the independent female. Horror films have come under attack for their part in portraying women as helpless females being hunted by sadistic men or monsters who represent men. Castle rarely chose this route for his films and in fact, his women were often strong, independent and sometimes even capable of murder themselves.

Macabre features several independent women including the nurse Polly and the doctor's sister-in-law who is blind, but lives life to the fullest until she dies during a botched abortion. *In House on Haunted Hill* and *The Tingler*, Vincent Price's wives are both devious women who try to murder their husbands.

Emily is the murderous female taking center stage in *Homicidal* and Joan Crawford also fills that spot in *Strait-Jacket* until the end of the film when it is revealed that her daughter is the real killer. *The Old Dark House* also features a murderous female and strong independent women are also featured in *The Night Walker*.

In *13 Frightened Girls* and *I Saw What You Did*, the young girls are menaced by killers, but they do prove to be worthy opponents and steer away from filling the standard helpless female role.

Other Common Denominators

Whether it is simply the genre he chose to work in or something more sinister at work, various other images are found throughout Castle's body of work during this period. Perhaps it can be written off as good scare tactics, but it is interesting to note some other common bonds between his films.

Severed heads and decapitation were depicted in numerous Castle classics. *House on Haunted Hill*, *13 Ghosts*, *Homicidal* and *Strait-Jacket* all feature at least one severed head, while most show several.

Castle's own inabilities as a child left him unable to participate in sports and made him feel worthless and may have led him to the use of disabled characters in many of his films. This may not be the case, but disabled characters were featured in numerous films, including the blind daughter in *Macabre*, the deaf mute woman in *The Tingler*, the mute housekeeper in *House on Haunted Hill*, the wheelchair-bound nurse in *Homicidal*, the disfigured servant in *Mr. Sardonicus*, and the blind husband in *The Night Walker*.

The death of both his parents may have played a role in the number of deaths in Castle horrors. Most often, two major characters died in each William Castle horror. The father-in-law and the doctor in *Macabre*; Annabelle Loren and her lover in *House on Haunted Hill*; The deaf mute woman and her husband Ollie in *The Tingler*; The uncle and the lawyer in *13 Ghosts*; The chaplin and the wheelchair-bound nurse in *Homicidal*; the father and son in *Mr. Sardonicus*; the husband and his lawyer in *The Night Walker*; and the wife and the neighbor in *I Saw What You Did*.

In *Strait-Jacket*, Joan Crawford murders her husband and his lover in the beginning and later her daughter murders the farmhand and the doctor. The film also includes one other murder, but it only serves as a lead to the climactic finale and in fact the finale is an attempt to murder all the parents in the film as Diane Baker's character kills her fiance's father then goes after his mother, and her own mother, Joan Crawford.

As mentioned, it was rare for a Castle picture to feature parents and often, as in *Strait-Jacket*, the parental figures that were included in the pictures ended up as murder victims. Two fathers in *Macabre*; Vincent Price's wives all died mysteriously in *House on Haunted Hill*; the uncle in *13 Ghosts*; the wheelchair-bound nurse who raised the killer in *Homicidal*; the father in *Mr. Sardonicus*; and both the father of Joan Crawford's daughter and as mentioned earlier, the daughter's finance's father in *Strait-Jacket*.

Castle's imagery within his films has occasionally been subject to discussion. The director himself told *Cinemafantastique* magazine in 1975 that he was amazed to find his films were "being treated with increasing respect, and taken very seriously today at the universities where they study them."

In fact, while Castle is often regarded as camp and schlock in the United States, his worked is held in higher regard in Europe. Castle himself took the analysis in stride and tried to explain it in one interview, saying, "It's a very strange thing. I definitely feel that possibly in my unconscious I was trying to day something...I never expected that they would put under a microscope pictures that I made in the 50s and 60s and look for hidden meanings. Nevertheless, that is what is happening...And I think about inner meaning, truly, it is possible that deeply buried within my unconscious was the feeling of trying to say something."

Under the Influence

Horror has been around a long time and the industry has a wealth of talent to consider when looking back at the genre as a whole. Many directors, writers and others involved in the creation of horror have a long list of people who they call influences. Screen greats like Lon Chaney, Vincent Price and Bela Lugosi, directors and producers like Hitchcock, Tod Browning, Roger Corman and a host of others are names that often come to mind. William Castle is another name that's also mentioned.

Many directors and horror buffs admit Castle's gimmicks were their lure to his films and that his work made a lasting impression on them. John Landis, Joe Dante, Robert Zemeckis and John Waters all have fond memories of Castle's films and his flair for gimmickry.

Movie Memories

"There are many great, wonderful horror films that were made in the 50s and 60s," Landis said in an interview. "The vast majority though are dreck, and there's great enjoyment in that too." Landis' own first film, called *Schlock*, paid tribute to the many of the low-budget horror films of the 50s and 60s.

Dante recalled seeing *13 Ghosts*. "I remember 3-D ghosts, where you had Ghost Viewers. The idea was that when the people on the screen saw the ghosts, you could put on your Ghost Viewer."

But Dante once admitted that his favorite Castle film came in 1961. "Mr. Sardonicus was the first interactive motion picture where, as you came into the theater, you were given fluorescent cards," said Dante explaining the gimmick of the Punishment Poll. "Of course, there was only one ending," he added.

"And we were all morons," joked John Landis. "We were all going thumbs down, thumbs down and, sure enough, he died."

Robert Zemeckis, in an article he authored for Film Comment in early 1995 considered Castle, "a great producer, obviously, but also a great director." He even admitted Castle's films "were a big influence on Death Becomes Her and the Tales of the Crypt series."

Dante's tribute to Castle came in 1993 when he released Matinee. Starring John Goodman as the film's main character, Lawrence Woolsey is a B-movie mogul whose campy horror pictures are promoted through gimmickry like wiring seats with buzzers and having ghouls soar over audiences.

Another earlier Dante film, Gremlins 2, also stole a Castle gimmick when, similar to The Tingler, the film appears to stop in midstream and the gremlins begin to make shadow puppets in the screen's light.

Perhaps, most of all, it was John Waters who was affected by Castle's brand of filmmaking. "I was obsessed by William Castle. I wanted to be William Castle. William Castle was god," wrote Waters. And Waters' tribute to Castle came in the form of Polyester. The film, released in 1981, brought the gimmick back to life when Waters promoted the film's process "Odorama," in which he gave out scratch and sniff cards to moviegoers before each showing.

Waters even wrote the forward to the rerelease of Castle's autobiography in 1992 writing, "When I was a kid I always wanted to sit on William Castle's lap, instead of Santa's, at Christmas and tell him what I wanted. Sometimes, I even prayed to William Castle. Seeing all his horror exploitation pictures…over and over wasn't enough. I wanted to live in a world that was as exciting as his horror exploitation gimmicks ('Emergo,' 'Percepto,' and 'Illusion-O.')"

Castle himself would probably be honored to know of the effect he had on these future filmmakers, but he once admitted he never really achieved the ultimate in gimmickry, which he considered would give moviegoers a movie for all their senses. "The audience would taste the fog drifting through a cemetery," Castle said. "They'd smell the freshly dug grave. They'd feel the touch of ghastly fingers."

Vincent Price, the star of two of his films, sometimes characterized Castle as a director without much talent. "He wasn't a great movie director," Price once said. "But he knew how to put these pictures together and he had wonderful, wild ideas." He also admitted, "He had a great sense of showmanship, and he was fun to work with."

The Legacy

Since his death, Castle's contribution to the film industry has become something of a legacy which has been illuminated by various events over the years. In addition to the films like *Matinee, Gremlins* and *Polyester* that have paid homage to William Castle in one way or another, and the rerelease of his memoirs in 1992, his brand of horror has been highlighted from time to time in other ways.

Film festivals in various major cities over the years have continued to keep his films alive. Showings in New York, San Francisco and other locales even dusted off his gimmicks, bringing back Percepto, Emergo and the Punishment Poll, among others. Even smaller film spots, like a movie house in Tampa, Florida brought back Illusion-O for a showing of *13 Ghosts*.

In addition, several film noir festivals have created new interest in some of his earlier films. Thrillers like *When Strangers Marry* and *The Whistler* have been brought back to the big screen in recent years showing some of his early promise of things to come to a whole new audience.

In 1984 the American Film Institute paid tribute to the "shock-schlock director" with a double feature showing of *Strait-Jacket* and *House on Haunted Hill.* Appropriately enough, the films were shown on Halloween. In fact, the ghoulish holiday is the most common time of the year when Castle's horrific features find their way back to the big screen.

Few of the director's wealth of early films with Columbia Pictures are available on video and rarely, if ever, do they make their way onto television. However, over the last few years his legacy of horror classics have made their way onto video. While several key films are still missing, *House on Haunted Hill, The Tingler, Strait-Jacket, 13 Ghosts, The Night Walker* and *Rosemary's Baby* have been released giving a new generation a chance to view his brand of horror.

It's important to note that key films like *Macabre, Homicidal, Mr. Sardonicus* and numerous other features of Castle's career are rarely found on home video and some may even be deteriorating beyond repair. But fortunately, even some of these rare films have been known to appear on video from independent video producers for private collectors. Some of these films have ended up in public domain and with private collectors. Sellers now use the Internet and the World Wide Web to market large collections of B movies to other private collectors who are often eager to pay whatever the asking price for a chance to see a film they remember from their childhood. Or perhaps a chance to see a film they've only read about in books.

Macabre, 13 Frightened Girls, Homicidal, Mr. Sardonicus, The Spirit is Willing and occasionally others are offered through this underground market. It's been reported that the mainstream video industry has long ignored Castle's films simply because they don't play well without their gimmicks. Only the few with major celebrities like Vincent Price, Joan Crawford and Barbara Stanwyck have found their way to video because the interest in the stars themselves drives demand for the pictures.

Remakes and Imitations

In 1987 there was talk of a remake of *The Tingler*. One news story reported the film would have a budget of $3 to $4 million and for the release there was even talk of reviving Castle's buzzing seats gimmick, however, something happened to the project and it never materialized.

However, in 1988 another Castle film did resurface as a remake. *I Saw What You Did* was remade for television by director Fred Walton, best known for his 1979 thriller *When a Stranger Calls*. It was obvious the Castle film interested Walton as *When a Stranger Calls* followed a similar theme as a baby-sitting teen is menaced by a telephone caller. The Castle remake starred David and Robert Carradine and aired on CBS.

In 1997, another horror film, *I Know What You Did Last Summer*, once again brought comparisons to Castle's 1965 film because of the similar sounding title. And like Castle's films, the horror was panned by the critics, but stayed afloat at the box office because of the teen-age market looking for a good scare.

The success of recent films like *Scream* and *I Know What You Did Last Summer* have shown that the market for Castle's brand of horror still exists. Elements, images and themes are echoed in current films and continue to keep the legacy of William Castle alive.

In addition, in early 1999, Director Robert Zemeckis and Producer Joel Silver joined forces to form Dark Castle Entertainment, a film company created "in the spirit of William Castle." The company's aim is to produce mid-budget horror pictures, much like Castle did. In fact, the film company's first project was a remake of Castle's feature, *House on Haunted Hill*, with Castle's daughter Terry, as a co-producer. Terry Castle, who was a producer for Nickelodeon TV, re-launched William Castle Production as a tribute to the work of her father.

In Conclusion

As a director William Castle failed to earn the respect and admiration he longed for from his fans and his contemporaries and although his financial success at the box office helped replace this loss, the need for approval was something he struggled with his entire life. As a showman Castle earned attention as well as success, but it wasn't really until after his death that respect for his showmanship grew.

The body of work he leaves behind, in large part, awaits the discovery of a new generation of moviegoers. The absence of many of his films from video and their rare appearances on television and in theaters leaves many without the opportunity to experience his brand of horror and his enthusiasm for showmanship.

But for those who do have the opportunity to view his major successes like *The Tingler, House on Haunted Hill, Strait-Jacket,* and even *Rosemary's Baby,* it's important to keep in mind that the director's intentions were not to educate or inform, but simply to entertain. His flair for showmanship is rarely seen in the movie business today and the quest for huge box office payouts has resulted in an escalation of budgets, special effects and gore, but not in the level of entertainment.

The filmgoing experience has once again become a passive experience of sights and sounds on the screen before us. If William Castle were alive today, perhaps he'd have found a way, within the boundless offerings of technology today, to give us that ultimate movie experience. The chance to feel the fog drifting by us as we smell the freshly dug grave in the cemetery and feel the fingers of the living dead grasp us from beneath the seats.

We would line up to take part.

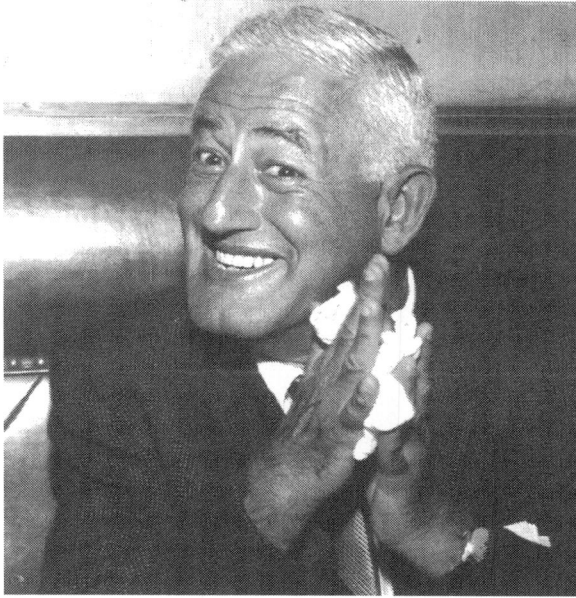

William Castle on a promotional tour in 1965. (Photo by Bill Cogan Photography)

William Castle's Filmography

The following is a chronological listing of William Castle's filmography. In Castle's early years at Columbia he was featured as an extra actor in numerous pictures and was involved in the production and editing of various studio films, many of which went uncredited. The list below are his credited features. Included are his role in each film as actor, writer, director or producer and the studio which released the film. Those films which are available on home video are noted as such, although that information is easily subject to change.

1937
It Could Happen To You
Actor
Republic Pictures

When Love Is Young
Actor
Universal Pictures

The Man Who Cried Wolf
Actor
Universal Pictures

1940
Music in My Heart
Dialogue Director
Columbia Pictures

He Stayed for Breakfast
Actor
Columbia Pictures

The Lady in Question
Actor
Columbia Pictures

1942
North To The Klondike
Writer
Universal Pictures

1943
Mr. Smug (Short film)
Director
Columbia Pictures

The Chance of a Lifetime
Director
Columbia Pictures

Klondike Kate
Director
Columbia Pictures

1944
The Whistler
Director
Columbia Pictures

When Strangers Marry (also
titled: *Betrayed*)
Director
Monogram Pictures

The Mark of the Whistler (also
titled: *The Marked Man*)
Director
Columbia Pictures

She's a Soldier Too
Director
Columbia Pictures

1945
Voice of the Whistler
Director/Writer
Columbia Pictures

Crime Doctor's Warning
Director
Columbia Pictures

Dillinger
Writer
Columbia Pictures

1946
Mysterious Intruder
Director
Columbia Pictures

Just Before Dawn
Director
Columbia Pictures

Crime Doctor's Man Hunt
Director
Columbia Pictures

The Return of Rusty
Director
Columbia Pictures

1947
Crime Doctor's Gamble
Director
Columbia Pictures

1948
The Lady From Shanghai
Co-Associate Producer
Columbia Pictures
(On video)

The Gentleman from Nowhere
Director
Columbia Pictures

Texas, Brooklyn and Heaven (also
titled: *The Girl from Texas*)
Director
United Artists

1949
Undertow
Director
Universal International

Johnny Stool Pigeon
Director
Universal International

1950
It's a Small World
Director/Writer
Eagle Lion Pictures

1951
Hollywood Story
Director
Universal International

The Fat Man
Director
Universal International

Cave of Outlaws
Director
Universal International

1953
Slaves of Babylon
Director
Columbia Pictures

Conquest of Cochise
Director
Columbia Pictures

Fort Ti
Director
Columbia Pictures

Serpent of the Nile
Director
Columbia Pictures

1954

Charge of the Lancers
Director
Columbia Pictures

Jesse James vs. the Daltons
Director
Columbia Pictures

The Saracen Blade
Director
Columbia Pictures

Masterson of Kansas
Director
Columbia Pictures

The Law vs. Billy the Kid
Director
Columbia Pictures

The Iron Glove
Director
Columbia Pictures

Drums of Tahiti
Director
Columbia Pictures

The Battle of the Rogue River
Director
Columbia Pictures

1955

New Orleans Uncensored
Director
Columbia Pictures

The Gun that Won the West
Director
Columbia Pictures

Duel on the Mississippi
Director
Columbia Pictures

The Americano
Director
Columbia Pictures
(On video)

1956

Uranium Boom
Director
Columbia Pictures

The Houston Story
Director
Columbia Pictures

1957

Men of Annapolis
Producer
Syndicated anthology TV series

1958
Macabre
Producer/Director
Allied Artists

1959
House on Haunted Hill
Producer/Director
Allied Artists
(On video)

The Tingler
Producer/Director
Columbia Pictures
(On video)

1960
13 Ghosts
Producer/Director
Columbia Pictures
(On video)

1961
Mr. Sardonicus
Producer/Director
Columbia Pictures
(On video)

Homicidal
Producer/Director
Columbia Pictures

1962
Zotz!
Producer/Director
Columbia Pictures
(On video)

1963
The Old Dark House
Producer/Director
Columbia Pictures

13 Frightened Girls (also titled:
The Candy Web)
Producer/Director
Columbia Pictures

1964
Strait-Jacket
Producer/Director
Universal International
(On video)

1965
The Night Walker
Producer/Director
Universal International
(On video)

I Saw What You Did
Producer/Director
Universal International

1966
Let's Kill Uncle
Producer/Director
Universal International

1967
The Spirit is Willing
Producer/Director/Actor
Paramount Pictures

The Busy Body
Producer/Director
Paramount Pictures

1968
Project X
Producer/Director
Paramount Pictures

Rosemary's Baby
Producer/Actor
Paramount Pictures
(On video)

1969
Riot
Producer
Paramount Pictures

1972
Ghost Story (Anthology TV series; retitled *Circle of Fear*)
Producer
NBC

1973
Circle of Fear (Anthology TV series)
Producer
NBC

1974
Shanks
Director/Actor
Paramount Pictures

The Sex Symbol (TV movie)
Actor
ABC

1975
Bug
Producer/Writer
Paramount Pictures
(On video)

The Day of the Locust
Actor
Paramount Pictures
(On video)

1976
Shampoo
Actor
Paramount Pictures
(On video)

About the Author

John W. Law is an editor and journalist whose work has appeared in newspapers, magazines and books. In all, he has worked on the staffs of six daily, three weekly and several monthly publications. He has also been an editor of several books by other authors. As a freelance writer his work has appeared in magazines and newspapers. He frequently writes on the film and entertainment industry. His first book, *Curse of the Silver Screen—Tragedy & Disaster Behind the Movies* was published in 1998 by Aplomb Publishing.

Bibliography

Books

Barker, Clive. *Clive Barker's A-Z of Horror.* 1997. New York. HarperCollins Publishers.

Brode, Douglas. *Lost Films of the Fifties.* 1991. New York. Carol Publishing Group.

Caesar, Sid (With Bill Davidson). *Where Have I Been?* 1982. New York. Crown Publishers Inc.

Castle, William. *Step Right Up—I'm Gonna Scare the Pants off America.* 1976. New York. Pharos Books.

Considine, Shaun. *Bette & Joan: The Divine Feud.* 1989. New York. Dell Publishing.

Drosnin, Michael. *Citizen Hughes.* 1985. New York. Bantam Books.

Diorio, Al. *Barbara Stanwyck.* 1983. New York. Coward-McCann Inc.

Eames, John Douglas. *The MGM Story.* 1990. New York. Portland House.

Finler, Joel W. *The Hollywood Story*. 1988. New York. Crown Publishers, Inc.

Guiles, Fred Lawrence. *Joan Crawford: The Last Word*. 1995. New York. Birch Lane Press.

Kapsis, Robert E. 1992. *Hitchcock: The Making of a Reputation*. Chicago. The University of Chicago Press.

Laguardia, Robert and Arceri, Gene. *Red: The Tempestuous Life of Susan Hayward* . 1985. New York. Macmillan Publishing Company.

Leaming, Barbara. *Polanski*. 1981. New York. Simon and Schuster.

Leaming, Barbara. *If This Was Happiness*. 1989. New York. Viking. Madsen, Axel. Stanwyck. 1994. New York. HarperCollins Publishers.

Leigh, Janet (with Christopher Nickens). *Psycho: Behind the Scenes of the Classic Thriller*. 1995. New York. Harmony Books.

McBride, Joseph. *Frank Capra: The Catastrophe of Success*. 1992. New York. Simon & Schuster.

McCarty, John. *The Fearmakers*. 1994. New York. St. Martin's Press.

McCarty, John. *The Modern Horror Film*. 1990. New York. Carol Publishing Group.

McCarty, John. *Psychos*. 1986. New York. St. Martin's Press.

Nelson, Nancy. *Evenings With Cary Grant*. 1991. New York. Warner Books.

Newquist, Roy. *Conversations With Joan Crawford.* 1980. New York. The Citadel Press.

Quirk, Lawrence J. *The Films of Joan Crawford.* New York. 1971. Citadel Press,Inc.

Schoell, William. *Stay Out of the Shower.* 1985. New York. Dembner Books.

Skal, David. *The Monster Show.* 1994. New York. Penguin Books.

Smith, Ella. *Starring Miss Barbara Stanwyck.* 1974. New York. Crown Publishers Inc.

Spoto, Donald. T*he Dark Side of Genius: The Life of Alfred Hitchcock* . 1983. New York. Ballantine Books.

Spoto, Donald. T*he Art of Alfred Hitchcock.* 1992. New York. Anchor Books.

Sternfield, Jonathan. *The Look of Horror.* 1990. New York. Moore & Moore Publishing.

Thomas, Bob. *Joan Crawford.* 1978. New York. Bantam Books.

Thompson, David. *Rosebud: The Story of Orson Welles.* 1996. New York. Alfred A. Knopf, Inc.

Waters, John. *Crackpot.* 1983. New York. Macmillan Publishing Company.

Magazines, Newspapers and Transcripts

Adler, Renata. "Screen: 'Rosemary's Baby,' a Story of Fantasy and Horror," *The New York Times.* June 13, 1968.

Archer, Eugene. "Double Bill Opens." *The New York Times.* July 27, 1961.

Archer, Eugene. "Double Horror Bill." *The New York Times.* October 31, 1963.

Archer, Eugene. "Tom Poston in Zotz!" *The New York Times.* October 4, 1962.

Bargreen, Melinda. "Theater Envy—Seattle May Turn Green as Tacoma Converts and Old Movie Palace into a Concert Hall." *The Seattle Times.* March 31, 1991.

Barrios, Gregg. "In Search of the Last Starlet." *Los Angeles Times.* January 1, 1989.

Barrios, Gregg. "Rediscovering the Last Starlet." *Los Angeles Times.* January 8, 1989.

Barson, Michael. "From Hackwork to Highbrow Horror." *The New York Times.* August 13, 1995.

Brottman, Mikita. Ritual, "Tension and Relief: The Terror of 'The Tingler.'" *Film Quarterly.* June 22, 1997.

Brown, Jeff and Roberts, Alison. "Tributes Pour in to Master of Horror." *The Times.* October 27, 1993.

Brown, Joe. "Tricks and Treats." *The Washington Post.* October 24, 1984.

Calta, Louis. "Leave It To The Girls." *The New York Times.* September 12, 1963.

Canby, Vincent. "Screen: Jim Brown Leads Prison Riot." *The New York Times*. January 26, 1969.

Craft, Dan. "Diabolique." *The Pantagraph*. August 15, 1997.

Crowther, Bosley. "Screen: Somnambulists." *The New York Times*. January 21, 1965.

Cuthbert, David. "Price Still Right in Sketchy 'Bio.'" *The Times-Picayune*. October 13, 1997.

Eddy, Steve. "B-Movie Director Castle Looks Back in 'Step Right Up.'" *The Orange County Register*. April 12, 1992.

Eder, Bruce. "Into the Spirits of '50s Gimmicks." *Newsday*. September 9, 1988.

Eder, Richard. "Screen: Poisonous 'Bug.'" *The New York Times*. September 18, 1975.

Farber, Stephen. "Alex North and His Oscar Make Musical Movie History." *The New York Times*. March 30, 1986.

Farber, Stephen. "'Jaws' and 'Bug'—The Only Difference is the Hype." *The New York Times*. August 24, 1975.

Feeney, Mary K. "Bugs Take Over the Movies: Is It Earth Next?." *The Ottawa Citizen*. September 2, 1997

Goldstein, Patrick. "Hollywood Signs: Controversial Films." *Los Angeles Times*. August 7, 1988.

Jackson, Kevin. "They Came from Beyond the Pale: Matinee's Shamelessly Vilgar Hero is a Z-Grade Horror Movie Producer of the 60s. But Which One?" *The Independent*. June 11, 1993.

Kelleher, Terry. "Film Forum 2's Summer Festival Is a Real Chiller." *Newsday*. August 9, 1991.

Kronke, David. "Master of the Gimmick." *Chicago Tribune*. February 11, 1993.

La Badie, Donald. "New Holocaust Film Predates Spielberg's 'List' By Four Years." *The Commercial Appeal* (Memphis). April 23, 1994.

Libman, Norma. "At Home in the South with Bailey White." *The Tennessean*. April 24, 1996.

Lomax, Sondra. "Speaking Well of Marcel." *Austin American-Statesman*. March 21, 1996.

Maslin, Janet. "There's A Horror Movie in Here!" *The New York Times*. January 29, 1993.

Myers, Gay Nagle. "Marina Cay Become the Stand-In for the 'Republic of Cuervo." *Travel Weekly*. April 1, 1996.

Noe, Denise. "What Kind of Woman Makes a Good Man? The 'Homicidal'-ly Bent Gender of Joan Marshall." *Chrysalis Quarterly*. Vol. 1, No. 7, 1994.

Price, Michael H. "Moviemaker Revisits His 60s Fright-Film Salad Days in 'Matinee'." *Star Tribune*. February 13, 1993

Rickey, Carrie. "Vincent Price Testimonial: A Gentle Man Who Scared Us Silly." *The Philadelphia Inquirer*. October 28, 1993.

Rickey, Carrie. "A Major Retrospective Sheds Light on Columbia Pictures." *The New York Times*. August 28, 1983.

Robbins, Wayne. "The Mainstreaming of John Waters." *Newsday*. April 6, 1990.

Rosenfield, Paul. "Saluting Stanwyck: A Life on Film." *Los Angeles Times*. April 5, 1987.

Scott, Vernon. "A Weekend With Vincent Price." U.P.I. July 9, 1990.

Severin, Steven. "Style: Men in Frocks." *The Guardian*. August 20, 1997.

Smith, Peter. "Marceau: Magician of Mime." *St. Petersburg Times*. February 26, 1988.

Staff. "The Gimmicks of William Castle." *The Times-Picayune*. February 6, 1993.

Staff. "The Tingler." *The Pantagraph*. July 18, 1997.

Staff. "William Castle, 63, Movie Producer." *The New York Times*. June 2, 1977.

Staff. "Obituaries, William Castle." Associated Press. June 2, 1977.

Staff. "How To Suceed in Hollywood Without Really Filming." *The New York Times*. July 5, 1981.

Staff. "Flashblacks." *The Vancouver Sun*. June 26, 1993.

Staff. "Klein-Schloss." *The New York Times*. November 1, 1926.

Staff. "Producer William Castle Dies at 63." *The Los Angeles Times*. June 3, 1977.

Stanley, John. "Screenwriter Charlie Haas Wired For a First-Hand Thrill." *The San Francisco Chronicle*. January 24, 1993.

Stanely, John. "Black September." *The San Francisco Chronicle*. September 8, 1990.

Stanley, John. "Roxie Renews Series." *The San Francisco Chronicle*. March 29, 1992.

Staten, Vince. "'Matinee' Pays Tribute to the Sultan of Scream." *The Courier-Journal*. June 26, 1993.

Streitfeld, David. "The State of the Art." *The Washington Post*. December 29, 1991.

Tallmer, Jerry. "Meet the Morbid Master Once Again." *The Record*. August 9, 1994.

Thomas, Kevin. "Movies of the Week." *Los Angeles Times*. May 15, 1988.

Thomas, Kevin. "Movies of the Week." *Los Angeles Times*. October 4, 1987.

Thompson, Douglas. "Manson: 'I'm Still Waiting To Kill'," *Sunday Mirror*. July 31, 1994.

Thompson, Howard. "Two Mild Shockers." *The New York Times*. July 24, 1958.

Thompson, Howard. "The Tingler." *The New York Times*. March 10, 1959.

Thompson, Howard. "Screen: New Double Bill." *The New York Times*. March 12, 1959.

Thompson, Howard. "Thriller Double Bill." *The New York Times*. July 22, 1965.

Thompson, Howard. "Screen: 'Let's Kill Uncle,' Bloodless Suspense Yarn." *The New York Times*. November 19, 1966.

Thompson, Howard. "'Warning Shot' and 'The Busy Body.'" *The New York Times*. June 8, 1967.

Torgerson, Dial. "Sharon Tate, Four Others Murdered," *Los Angeles Times*. August 10, 1969.

Weiler, A.H. "Marceau in Dual Roles in 'Shanks.'" *The New York Times*. September 10, 1974.

Westbrook, Bruce. "Beyond the Villain." *The Houston Chronicle*. October 24, 1993.

Wire Services. "A Tingler Remake in High Tech." *The Record*. June 19, 1987.

Wloszczyna, Susan. "'Matinee' Idol William Castle's Horror Show." *USA Today*. February 17, 1993.

Zemeckis, Robert. "Guilty Pleasures' Favorite Not-So-Good Films." *Film Comment*. January 1995.

Index

Printed in Poland
by Amazon Fulfillment
Poland Sp. z o.o., Wrocław